ENTREPRENEURSHIP DEVELOPMENT

ENTREPRENEURSHIP DEVELOPMENT

An Analytical Study

By

Thaduri Balaraju

AKANSHA PUBLISHING HOUSE
NEW DELHI-110 059 (INDIA)

AKANSHA PUBLISHING HOUSE
R-37B, Vani Vihar, Uttam Nagar
New Delhi-110059
Phones: 56065579, 9811582579
Email: ektabooks@yahoo.com

Entrepreneurship Development

First Published 2004

ISBN 81-87606-49-5

PRINTED IN INDIA

Published by M.P. Misra for Akansha Publishing House, New Delhi-110059 and Printed at Tarun Offset Press, Delhi.

Dedicated

to

My Beloved Parents

Foreword

The birth pangs of a New Society are mediated through the midwifery of entrepreneurship. Entrepreneurship can be likened to leadership in business and in developing societies like India, it plays a crucial role in the process of social change. It is now a well recognized fact that physical capital formation alone cannot bring about economic growth in a society. Nay, it is human capital formation that ultimately acts as the dividing line between developed and developing nations. Entrepreneurship, being the fulcrum around which human capital grows, has played a decisive role in shaping the future of many a society. It is in this genre, I find Dr. Balaraju's book on Entrepreneurship Development: An Analytical Study, which shows welcome features on a theme familiar to social scientists.

As a scientist trained in pharmaceutical sciences, I had the advantage of closely observing at the way in which pharmaceutical firms were provided with innovative leadership at the nascent stage of the development of the pharmaceutical industry. The phenomenal growth of pharmaceutical units bears testimony to the role of entrepreneurship in the growth of an otherwise risky business. As I leafed through the research study of Dr. Balaraju, I am impressed by the diligent methodology adopted for this study. I am of the opinion that a State like Andhra Pradesh can surge through a faster tempo of economic development if a band of new entrepreneurs emerges to take the reins of industrial leadership in Andhra Pradesh, especially in economically backward regions, such as Telangana, where the author had conducted his field study. As these studies will highlight the part assigned to entrepreneurship in social transformation, I am delighted to see Dr. Balaraju including Adilabad district, which is the least developed district in Telangana region, in his study.

As a layman in the subject of business management, I had gone through the book which is based on the doctoral dissertation of the author. A pertinent point made in this study is the primacy to be accorded to entrepreneurship development programmes as entrepreneurship, though ingenious in nature, also requires some nurturing. It stresses the three components of successful entrepreneurship, namely, location, target group and enterprise. Many a entrepreneur could correctly identify these components and a right mix resulted in achieving success. Today, in a State like Andhra Pradesh, a pharmaceutical company, Dr. Reddy's Laboratories achieving a breakthrough in U.S.A. by bagging a patent is a clear indicator to the role of entrepreneurship. An interesting finding that emerges from this study is that entrepreneurs in small scale industries could be thriving and the firms that had a working capital in the range of Rs. 5 to 15 lakhs could acquire some prominence due to the positive association between their working capital and profit making capacity. Caste background and education are often found to be playing a significant role in risk taking nature of entrepreneurship, but this study highlights how entrepreneurs from S.T. category, though economically backward could succeed in improving their profit range over time. The district-wise analysis also brings out the contribution that DICs can make for the growth of entrepreneurship.

In the initial chapters, the theoretical insights on the prominent role of entrepreneurship had been highlighted by the researcher. Besides these findings, Dr. Balaraju has made a meticulous district-wise cross-section study of entrepreneurship in this book, which will open new vistas of research, in this ever interesting field. I hope that this book will kindle interest among the researchers in this specialized subject and I earnestly feel that this book on entrepreneurship development will be a welcome addition to the growing multi-faceted studies on entrepreneurship as well as, its development. I commend the author for bringing out such a good piece of research work that will be useful for current research, but can also act as a benchmark for future research.

—Prof. Chandrakant Kokate
Vice-Chancellor
Kakatiya University,
Warangal (A.P.)

Vidyaranyapuri, Warangal

Acknowledgements

At the outset I express my deep gratitude to my teacher and supervisor Prof. Ojha Ghanshyam Das, Professor and former Dean, Head and Chairman, Dept. of Commerce & Management, Kakatiya University, Warangal for his encouragement and personal affection. Without his guidance and inducement, this work would not have come to its successful completion.

I owe a deep sense of gratitude to Prof. Chandrakant Kokate, Vice-Chancellor, Kakatiya University, for his inspiration as well as for writing a Foreword to this book. I am indebted to Prof. Vidyavathi, former Vice-Chancellor, Kakatiya University, Warangal, who had been a constant source of inspiration to me for the completion of this work.

I am thankful to the Senior most teacher of the department, Prof. A. Shankaraiah and other senior teachers Prof. K. Rajeshwar Rao, Prof. G. Krishna Murthy and Prof. V. Gangadhar who had been advising me at various stages of this work.

I am grateful to Dr. Sudharshan, Dean, Faculty of Commerce & Business Management for his support and guidance. I am indebted to Dr. Ravi Prakash Singarvelu, Head, Dept. of Commerce & Business Management for the keen interest he evinced in my work as he had advised me in the topic selection and in the gathering information from various sources. I am thankful to Prof. G. Narasimha Murthy, Chairman, Board of Studies in Commerce & Business Management who had been a constant source of encouragement to me. I thank

Prof. V. Gopal Reddy, Principal, Univ. Arts & Science College, K.U. Warangal for his support to me in the completion of this work.

I owe my gratitude to Prof. B. Venkata Ratnam for his guidance at various stages of this work. I am thankful to Prof. R. Natarajan and Dr. K. Sayulu, Vice-Principal, University College, K.U., for their encouragement. I am thankful to all my teachers in the Department at Univ. College and University Arts & Science College, PG. College, Subedari, Hanamkonda.

I shall be failing in my duty if I do not mention the names of Prof. C. Siva Rama Krishna Rao, Dept. of Economics and Prof. N. Linga Murthy, Principal, Univ. College, for their help and encouragement.

I am thankful to Dr. N. Rajendra Prasad, Lecturer in Statistics for his help in statistical work. I owe my special thanks to Mrs. Ojha Vijaya Laxmi, Mrs. C. Nageswari and Mrs. Bhanumathi Singarvelu who had been a source constant inspiration to me.

I am beholden to my father Late Sri T. Lingaiah and my mother Smt. Ilamma who had moulded me to this stage and I am every thankful to them for their love and affection. My wife Mrs. T Anitha had borne all the brunt of my work and this work would not have been completed without her cooperation and encouragement. I have received constant encouragement from my sister Smt. E. Laxmi and brother-in-law Sri E. Rajaiah who have lent support to me at the various stages of this work.

My thanks are due in no small measure to Mr. R Mahidhar Reddy, who had done all the completion work. I am thankful to Mr. V. Pruthivi Raju, CCT, Dept. of Commerce & Business Management, for his cooperation at various stages in this work. I shall be once again failing in my duty if I do not thank all the entrepreneurs, who cooperated with me in the data collection. I once again thank all the research scholars in the Department and all my well wishers in the University.

Contents

Abbreviations Used

APIIC	-	Andhra Pradesh Industrial Infrastructure Corporation
APSFC	-	Andhra Pradesh State Finance Corporation
APIDC	-	Andhra Pradesh Industries Development Corporation
APSSIDC	-	Andhra Pradesh Small Scale Industries Development Corporation
APITCO	-	Andhra Pradesh Industrial and Technical Consultancy Organisation Ltd.
ADB	-	Asian Development Bank
DIC	-	District Industries Centres
DER	-	Debt Equity Ratio
EPZ	-	Export Processing Zone
EDII	-	Entrepreneurship Development Institute of India
EDP	-	Entrepreneurship Development Programme
IDBI	-	Industrial Development Bank of India
ICICI	-	Industrial Credit Investment Corporation of India
NIESBUD	-	National Institute for Entrepreneurship and Small Business Development

NISIET	-	National Institute of Small Industries and Extension Training
NSIC	-	National Small Industries Corporation
SSI Sector	-	Small Scale Industries Sector
SIDBI	-	Small Industries Development Bank of India
SIET	-	Small Industry Extension Training Institute
SOL	-	Standard Organic Ltd.
SISI	-	Small Industry Service Institutes
TCOS	-	Technical Consultancy Organisations
TSNES	-	Technicians and New Entrepreneurs Scheme of Finance
WB	-	World Bank

1
Introduction

Entrepreneurship is considered as an important pre-requisite for economic development. Entrepreneurs, who imbue the quality of entrepreneurship, play a major role not only in organising production, but in a broader sense promote the process of economic development. According to Joseph Schumpeter the function of an entrepreneur is to reform or revolutionalise the pattern of production by exploiting an invention or more generally an untried technological possibility for producing a new commodity or producing an old one in a new way, by opening up a new source of supply of raw materials or a new outlet for product by organising an industry. To undertake such new things is not an easy task and constitutes a distinct economic function, first because they lie outside of the routine tasks which every body understands and secondly, because the environment resists in many ways that vary according to social conditions from simple refusal either to finance or to buy new things to physical attack on the man who tries to produce it. To act with confidence beyond the range of familiar beacons and to overcome that persistence requires aptitudes that are present in only a small fraction of the population and that define the entrepreneurial type as well as the entrepreneurial function.[1]

Entrepreneur's role, though less glamorous at times, great or small is just another form of individual leadership acting by virtue of personal force and personal responsibility for success. His position is threatened as soon as this function in the social process loses its importance, and no less if this is due to cessation of the social needs it served than if those needs are being served by other, more impersonal methods.

But as the social needs multiply the role of entrepreneur becomes apparent and entrepreneurship as such acquires importance in such a society. As most of the developing economies are in a process transition, entrepreneurship, some times has to be inculcated and its development, often undertaken by the state also can be a harbinger of economic development. As entrepreneurship is expected to play a major role in the process of development, a brief historical note will highlight how this concept had developed over time.

The usual manner in which factors of production are mentioned in economic theory consist of four factors namely land, labour, capital and entrepreneur. But there are other economists who tried to highlight the fact that if we treat the entrepreneur as a distinct factor of production, receiving his marginal product, we cannot logically equate this marginal product to pure profit. Pure profit is either the marginal product of some factor or it is a non-imputed residual. Hence the marginal product of entrepreneurship cannot be pure profit. But the difficulty is that we cannot precisely define the marginal product of a factor unless the factor is both infinitely divisible and strictly homogenous. In the case of entrepreneurship the usual practical compromises have to be carried to excessive lengths. If the entrepreneur is a person, a firm has room for only so many entrepreneurs and therefore entrepreneurs cannot be treated as members of a homogenous group. If entrepreneurship is a function, it cannot be finely divided in terms of some thing like entrepreneurial man hours as the fundamental units of supply. Therefore entrepreneurship is a function that fails to satisfy the conditions required to define a factor of production.[2]

Since entrepreneurship is a vital function in an economic

system characterised by private ownership of capital, economists, tried to analyse this concept in many ways.

Among the early economists Adam Smith did not distinguish it in any way between the capitalist as the provider of the 'stock' of the enterprise and the entrepreneur as the ultimate decision maker. Even in the early period when the corporate form of business organisation has been in vogue, the capitalist role of stock holders is sharply distinguished from the decision making role of managers and entrepreneurs. In the early phase of industrial revolution or before 1840 the prevalent form of business ownership in United Kingdom was the small to medium sized family firm, the capital funds being provided by the owner, his relatives or his friends. Hence the early economists failed to highlight a distinctive character of the entrepreneurial function.

But among the early economists it was Richard Cantillon who could foresee the entrepreneurial function, as he observed that discrepancies between demand and supply in a market create opportunities for some one to buy cheap and sell dear. He named people who take advantage of these unrealised profit opportunities' entrepreneurs', that is individuals who are willing to buy at a certain price and sell at an uncertain price. This entrepreneurship for Cantillon is the a matter of foresight and willingness to assume risk, which is not necessarily connected with the employment of labour in same productive process.[3] Therefore Cantillon left no doubt of the difference between the functions of the entrepreneur and those of the capitalist.

Another writer who attempted to define the entrepreneurial role is von Thunen. Thunen defined the gains of the entrepreneur as the income which is left over from the gross profits of a business operation after payment of

1. interest on invested capital
2. the wages of management and
3. an insurance premium against the calculable risk of losses.

The rewards of the entrepreneur, Thunen went on to say, are therefore the returns for incurring those risks which no insurance company will cover because they are unpredictable.

Since novel action is precisely the condition under which it is impossible to predict this probability of gain or loss, the entrepreneur is necessarily an inventor and explorer in his field. Another economist Frank Knight elaborated on Thunen's distinction between risk and uncertainty. According to him risks become an element of the cost of production, a deduction from and not a cause of profit or losses. The presence of the 'uncertainty' about the future may allow entrepreneurs to earn positive profits despite perfect competition, long run equilibrium and product exhaustion. But Schumpeter held a different opinion and he traced all economic changes to innovation and identified innovator with the entrepreneur. The entrepreneur is the source of all dynamic change in an economy and capitalist system for entrepreneur cannot be understood except in terms of the conditions giving rise to entrepreneurship. The entrepreneur in Schumpeter has a functional role which is not necessarily embodied in a single physical person and certainly not in a well defined group of people. The entrepreneur may be a capitalist or even a corporate manager but whether all these different functions are combined in one or more persons depends on the nature of capital markets and the form of industrial organisation.[4]

The modern view of an entrepreneur is mirrored by Peter Drucker, who described the entrepreneurial role as one of gathering and using resources, but added that 'resources, to produce results must be allocated to opportunities rather than to problems'. In Drucker's view entrepreneurship occurs when resources are redirected to progressive opportunities, not used to ensure administrative efficiency. This redirection of resources distinguishes the entrepreneurial role from that of the traditional management role.[5]

A recent definition given by Robert Ronstadt captures the essence of entrepreneurship. The definition is as follows:

> "Entrepreneurship is the dynamic process of creating incremental wealth. This wealth is created by individuals who assume the major risks in terms of equity, time, and / or career commitment of providing value for some product or service. The product or service itself may or may not be new or unique but value must somehow be infused by the entrepreneur by securing and allocating the necessary skills and resources."

The research on entrepreneurship shows that its nature is often a matter of individual perception. Karl Vesper had highlighted the different view points about entrepreneurs. Economists endorse Schumpeter's view point that entrepreneurs being resources together in unusual combinations to generate profits, Vesper found that psychologists view entrepreneurs in behavioural terms as achievement oriented individuals driven to seek challenges and new accomplishments. Corporate managers often view entrepreneurs as small business persons lacking the potential needed for corporate management. Hence Vesper suggests that in a market economy entrepreneurs can be viewed as pillars of industrial strength - the movers and shakers who constructively distrupt the status quo.[6]

Often a distinction may be made between small business persons and entrepreneurs. Individuals who simply substitute income by leaving jobs to operate local stores or independent service business are described as small business persons. But the term entrepreneur may be properly applied to those who incubate new ideas, start enterprises based on those ideas and provide added value to society based on their independent initiative. Distinguishing factors are that entrepreneurs have vision for growth, commitment to constructive change, persistence to gather. Necessary resources and energy to achieve unusual results. The small business persons may also exhibit, these characteistics, but only coincidently not as prerequisite to establishing an enterprise.[7]

Major changes are taking place all over the world, especially in business world. The challenge of turning an

Entrepreneurship do not have the time to think about failure as they consider it to be a mere passing event in the continuous journey to sucess. Entrepreneurship is all about the process of creating new organisations or small businesses offering something new to customers, employers or other stake holders by the entrepreneur. Entrepreneurship is also about innovation and change. Hence the entrepreneur having an idea of the business is not enough. They have to identify the market also. As the entrepreneuers face competition in domestic as well as international market, the present challenge is in identifying the global market. Hence the challenge is change.[8]

Presently the business world is in a situation where there is uncertainty, electronic high ways like the internet is giving chance to small entrepreneurs to compete with large and multinational companies on a more level playing field. It is no more possible to forecast prices, cost and interest rates as the changes are more frequent in the global market place. Technology also has a big role in creating uncertainties, because it is responsible for constantly changing the very features of dying business. Therefore today's entrepreneurs are that variety who are not only risk takers, but are also flexible, dynamic and have the ability to create change.

In this new environment entrepreneurs who start small businesses are able to enter the capital market with their innovative ideas. Therefore as the entrepreneurship is considered as a trait certain programmes are being initiated to develop certain individuals as entrepreneurs. As this novel feature is becoming important in the present day business world, the topic chosen for research is "Entrepreneurship Development in Andhra Pradesh - An Analytical Study".

Methodology

In this study an attempt is made to analyse the concept of entrepreneurship and entrepreneurship development programmes in general and those initiated by the state of Andhra Pradesh. Further, entrepreneurs operating either small businesses or small scale/tiny units will be selected for conducting a study on their traits. The methodology adopted in this study will be given here under.

Objectives

The objectives of study are:

1) To analyse the concept of entrepreneurship;
2) To review the empirical studies on entrepreneurship,
3) To trace the entrepreneurship development programmes and to assess the impact of these programmes on industrial sector in general and small scale industry sector in particular;
4) To explain the socio-cultural profile of entrepreneurship,
5) To make a probe into the achievements of entrepreneurs in terms of certain economic indicators and
6) To study the behavioural aspects of entrepreneurs in promoting their business.

The hypotheses that will be tested here will be as follows:

1. Entrepreneurship depends on the innovative ability of the entreprenurs.
2. The role of entrepreneurs depends on the socio-cultural factors that mould the entrepreneurs.
3. Successful entrepreneurship depends on profit making nature of the entrepreneurs.

The reasearch design for the study is ex-post facto experimental design. In this technique the varying influence of the identical factors is usually chosen. Here in this study as more factors may be influencing entreprenerurship, these factors will be analysed, especially laying stress on innovation and change. Usually two groups are chosen for such a study but here the same group before and after change is studied.

Sample Design

The sampling method chosen for the above research design is mutlistage sampling method. Initially four districts in the state of Andhra Pradesh had been chosen. These districts are situated in the Telengana Region of Andhra Pradesh. The four districts are Adilabad, Karimnagar, Khammam and Warangal. At the second stage in each district different production processes have been studied and the processes that have attracted more industrial units have been considered in this study. In the next stage among these processes a sample of units had been chosen based on the investment of fixed as well as working captial that had been functioning with some success in Adilabad, Karimanagar, Khammam and Warangal .

Data Base

The primary data has been collected with the help of a structured questionnaire administered to 150 respondents who are organising small scale units in the four districts. Besides administering the questionnaire, oral interviews were also conducted to collect the data. The secondary data had been collected from books, periodicals, government reports, and unpublished dissertations.

Data Analysis

The primary data were analysed with the help of two way and three way cross breaks. Further percentages have been calculated and statistical tools like tests of hypothesis had been conducted.

Limitations

As the researcher had been doing part- time teaching work, the data collection could be done only during the vacations. Further as the units are dispersed over a wide region it had been a time consuming process for serving the questionnaires and collecting the data from entrepreneurs.

In the first chapter on introduction, besides analysing the concept of entrepreneurship in its broad outline, the methodology adopted in this study is also presented.

A brief review of the literature on entrepreneurship is attempted in the second chapter.

The third chapter is on the Entrepreneurship Development programmes. In this chapter the institutional setup in the state of Andhra Pradesh for promoting entrepreneurship is analysed. Further a review of the studies on entreprenereship conducted is also given.

The socio-economic profile of the entrepreneurs in the sample chosen for study is presented in the fourth chapter. An assessment of the role of entrepreneur on the basis of certain indicators that influence the profitability of an organisation is the subject matter of the fifth chapter.

An attitudinal study of the behavioural patterns of entrepreneurs in the changing business environment is portrayed in the sixth chapter.

The conclusions and suggestions of this study are presented in the last chapter.

NOTES

1. Joseph A. Schumpeter, *Capitalism, Socialism and Democracy*, S. Chand & Company, New Delhi, 1980, p. 132.
2. Mark Blaug, *Economic Theory in Retrospect*, Cambridge University Press, 1997, pp. 440-441.
3. *Ibid.*, p. 442.
4. *Ibid.*, pp. 444-446.
5. David H. Hold, *Entrepreneurship*, Prentice Hall of India, New Delhi, 1998, p. 7.
6. *Ibid.*, pp. 8-9.
7. *Ibid.*, p. 11.
8. Siddharth G. Das, "Entrepreneurship in the 21st Century", *Indian Management*, June 1999.

2
Entrepreneurship: A Brief Survey of Literature

The concept of entrepreneurship has been around for a very longtime, but its resurgent popularity implies a sudden discovery.[1] Richard Cantillon is credited with giving the concept of entrepreneurship a central role in Economics. According to him Entrepreneurs consciously make decisions about resource allocations. They would always seek the best opportunities for using resources for the highest commercial yields.[2] Adam Smith spoke of the enterpriser in his *Wealth of Nations* as an individual who undertook the formation of an organisation for commercial purposes. He has ascribed to the entrepreneur the role of industrialist, but he also viewed entrepreneur as a person with unusual foresight who could recognise potential demand for goods and services. Another economist, Jean Baptiste Say described an entrepreneur as one who possessed certain arts and skills of creating new economic enterprises, yet a person who had exceptional insight into society's needs and was able to fulfill them.

Entrepreneur and His Role

A change in the connotation of an entrepreneur from captain of Industry to an elusive character, where the entrepreneur is characterised as one who garners profits at the expense of others had distorted the concept of entrepreneurship. The concept of entrepreneurship has been revised by an economist, Joseph Schumpeter. Schumpeter described entrepreneurship as a force in creative destruction, whereby established ways of doing things are distraught by the creation of new and better ways to get things done. Hence Schumpeter described entrepreneurship as a process and entrepreneurs as innovators who use the process to shatter the status quo through new combinations of resources and new methods of commerce.[3] Joseph A. Schumpeter thus writes: "The entrepreneur in an advanced economy is an individual who introduces something new in the economy a method of production not yet tested by experience in the branch of manufacture concerned, a product with which consumers are not yet familiar, a new source of raw-material or of new markets and the like".[4] He further states the entrepreneur's function is to "reform or revolutionise the pattern of production by exploiting an invention or more generally, an untried technological possibility for producing a new commodity or producing an old one in a new way, by opening up a new source of supply of materials or a new outlet for products.... Entrepreneurship, as defined, essentially consists in doing things that are not generally done in the ordinary course of business routine".[5]

Peter Drucker describes entrepreneurial role as one of gathering and using resources. But Drucker's view of entrepreneurship occurs when resources are redirected to progressive opportunities, not used to ensure administrative efficiency. This redirection of resources distinguishes the entrepreneurial role from that of the traditional management role.[6] Some other definitions of entrepreneurs are given by the following authors. Frank Young describes entrepreneur as a change agent. Noah Webster thinks entrepreneur is one who assumes the responsibility of the risk and management of business. Francis A. Walter observes that the true entrepreneur is one who is endowed with more than average capacities in the risk of organising and coordinating the various other factors of production.[7]

Karl Vesper found that psychologists tend to view entrepreneur in behavioural terms as achievement oriented individuals driven to seek challenges and new accomplishments. Hence he suggests in a market economy entrepreneurs can be viewed as pillars of industrial strength—the movers and the shakers who constructively disturb the status quo.[8]

The term 'entrepreneur' may be properly applied to those who incubate new ideas, and provide added value to society based on their independent initiative. The person who establishes a fast food franchise chain is called an entrepreneur, but the local restaurant owner is called a small business person. Distinguishing factors are that entrepreneurs have vision for growth, commitment to constructive change, persistence to gather necessary resources and energy to achieve unusual results. The small business person may exhibit these characteristics, but only coincidentally, not as a prerequisite to establishing an enterprise.[9]

The concept of entrepreneurship does not exclude managers in large organisation from being entrepreneurs if they combine resources in unusual ways to create innovative new product or services. However, because entrepreneurs take personal investment risks and corporate managers very rarely do, corporate entrepreneurship, some times referred to as entrepreneurship at has to be differentiated from the concept of entrepreneurship proper.

Entrepreneurship

Entrepreneurship is a process undertaken by an entrepreneur to augment his business interest. Thus Entrepreneurs do not emerge spontaneously on their own. Entrepreneurs appear to have been motivated by a combination and interaction of various factors. Thus entrepreneurship is influenced by a host of factors and in the recent years entrepreneurship became a fine art as it has evolved as a science of management and a catalytic tool of economic growth and development. Hence entrepreneurship as a process undertaken by an entrepreneur to augment his business interest involves innovation and creativity that will go towards establishing an enterprise. The qualities of entrepreneurship are his ability to discover and innovate opportunity and to organise an enterprise, thereby contributing to real economic growth. Entrepreneurship is a composite skill, the resultant of a mix of many qualities and traits—these include tangible factors such as imagination, readiness to take risk, ability to bring together and put to use other factors of production such as capital, labour, land, and also intangible factors such as the ability to mobilise scientific and technological advances. Therefore entrepreneurship is the propensity of mind to take calculated risk with confidence to achieve a predetermined business or industrial objective. In the words of A.H. Cole, entrepreneurship is the purposeful activity of an individual or a group of associated individuals undertaken to initiate, maintain or organise a profit oriented business unit for the production or distribution of economic goods and services.[10]

In other words entrepreneurship means the function of creating something new, organising and coordinating and undertaking risk and acting on economic uncertainty. Higgins defines the term entrepreneurship as a function of seeing investment and production opportunity, organising an enterprise to undertake a new production process, raising capital, hiring labour, arranging for the supply of raw materials and getting top managers for the day to day operation of the enterprise. Thus the entrepreneurship is the complex phenomenon and it is an attitude of mind which calls for calculated risks. Hence the true entrepreneur is one who can see possibility in a given situation where others see none and has the patience to work out the idea into schemes to which financial support can be provided. Therefore the simulation of entrepreneurship is a function of both internal and external factors.[11]

The small scale industry sector in a country like India is considered as an ideal nursery for the rapid growth and development of entrepreneurship. The man who will set up small Industry unit has to come from within the country and community and therefore they have a much greater impact on generating the right climate for successful entrepreneurship. Hence programmes for the developing of the entrepreneurship must recognise that alternately the change they see to induce his attitude is more than just providing information, land, or money. It is to provide new goals which will ensure for the risk taken a modest income but seeks bigger challenges in setting of and running their own business. The risks are greater but so are the rewards both in monetary sense and psychologically, in the feeling of confidence and pride it generates in a person.

According to Drucker the entrepreneurial management is the need of the hour, that is the society needs innovation and entrepreneurship in a normal, steady and ongoing basis.[12]

Entrepreneurship training in most countries of the world is being increasingly tried to promote local entrepreneurship and accelerate the base of small enterprise development. Recent studies conducted in USA suggest the positive link between economic development and entrepreneurship. But the developing economy also suffer from lack of proper consideration of current models of entrepreneurship development.

Plaschka and Welsch suggest that the development of entrepreneurship is the result of coordination of internal and external components facing the entrepreneurs. Internal components include factors such as individual characteristics of employees, financial resources and firm characteristics such as systems of production, organisation and marketing. External components include factors such as government taxes, laws, regulations and free trade policy, location, infrastructure and the existence of enterprise zones; the availability of skilled labour force; the presence of venture capital, government loans and grants and the presence of supporting institutions and systems, public and private partnerships, networking and cooperative support between entrepreneurs. The favourability and unfavourability of internal and external components can influence the entrepreneur's ability to create viable organisation.[13]

While the internal and external components that influence entrepreneurship are multifaceted in nature, it has not been thoroughly explored. Many writers could not provide a satisfactory analysis of either the role of entrepreneurship and its supply or the type of Schumpeterian entrepreneur, as pointed out by Baumol, is visually absent from the received theory of firm.

On the basis of the degree of innovative zeal, propensity to introduce change, and qualities of leadership displayed, entrepreneurs have been classified by 'Danhot' into four distinct types. The first one is innovating entrepreneurship which is aggressive in experimentation and always ready for putting attractive possibilities into practice. The second is imitative entrepreneurship distinguished by the preparedness to adopt successful innovations initiated by innovating entrepreneurs. The third category is Fabian entrepreneurship, characterised by greater caution and skepticism, which introduces changes only when the non-introduction leads to loss. The fourth category is the drone entrepreneurship which is characterised by refusal to try the new methods even at the risks of loss.[14]

Another classification of entrepreneurs from the development angle, has been attempted and these have been described briefly.

Prime Mover Type

The entrepreneurs falling in this category are those who set in motion a powerful sequence of development, growing, expanding and diversification oriented.

Manager Type

The entrepreneurs are more keen on keeping the unit

running, handles the environment effectively, but does not initiate development.

Minor Innovator Type

The entrepreneurs in this class, contribute to economic progress by finding better use of the society's resources although his contribution individually may be negligible.

Initiator Type

These entrepreneurs slowly enter the diffusion process of innovation and slowly development begins.

Satellite Type

The entrepreneurs prefer to be ancillaries to the parent or mother units, thus assuming a supplier role, and in the course of time they may emerge independent.

Local Trading Type

These entrepreneurs are mostly confined to local market, hesitant to try beyond that.

Collins and Moore have classified entrepreneurs into administrative and independent types. Individual divisions within already existing organisations are included in the category of administrative entrepreneurs. Smith has come up with two ideal types of entrepreneurs and named them c. .ft entrepreneurs (CE) and opportunity entrepreneurs (OE). According to Smith, the differences between the two classes of entrepreneurs are related to breadth of education and training, higher social awareness, involvement and ability to deal with economic and social environment and time orientation. Gilmore has reported that OE were found more often among successful entrepreneurs than among CE.

Hundal has attempted to classify entrepreneurs into distinct types based on the nature of industry they owned as fast progressive (textile, hosiery) and slow progressive (foundry, steel) industries. Hundal found significant differences among the entrepreneurs belonging to the two types of industries with regard to their individual and behavioural characteristics.

Venkatapathy proposed that entrepreneurs could possibly be classified as First Generation entrepreneurs and Second Generation Entrepreneurs. The classification stems from the results of various investigations carried out to study the psychological characteristics of the said cross-section of entrepreneurs before formulating them as distinct types.

Despite the existence of various types of entrepreneurs, the fact remains that the basic objective in developing entrepreneurship and multiplying these in the society, has been to generate productive human resources, mobilise and sustain the same in subsequent process of development. The spontaneity and continuity of the process would depend on the kind of people that can be promoted and groomed in the entrepreneurial career.[15]

Theories of Entrepreneurship

The entrepreneur in a small industrial sector need neither be a Schumpeterian innovator nor possess highly creative personality suggested by some writers. It is adequate if he can benefit from the experience of his fellow industrialists and can use his ingenuity and judgement to carefully study the economic environment and opportunity to take proper decisions. It should be recognised that supply of entrepreneurship is influenced by various factors and differs from country to country. Hence it is not possible to make any generalisation as regards the influences which act and react on economic activity and on entrepreneurship. But apart from Schumpeter there are others like Weber, Everett, E. Hagen, Thomas Cochran, Frank Young, John H. Kunkel and David McClelland who have given theories of entrepreneurship. In the Weberian system the motivating force for the entrepreneurial activity is provided by Calvinist ethic irrespective of the cultural background, personality type of the individual and the social environment in which he lives. Hence in this system the entrepreneurial energies are generated by following exogenously supplied religious belief, that is protestant ethic.

Hagen takes up the forces that will bring about social change and technological forces. By studying a number of countries in which there has occurred a transition from a traditional state to a modern state of continuing economic development, he draws an inference that an important factor initiating a change was some historic shift which caused some group or groups of leading elite who previously had a respected and valued place in the social hierarchy, to feel that they no longer were respected and valued. Hagen quotes the case of Japan where the Samurai were deprived of their traditional function and it was the lesser Samurai who played the innovators' role in Japan's industrial revolution. To put it in another way it is the social group that experienced withdrawal of status that turned to vigorous entrepreneurial activity. They are a group of individuals, creative, alienated from traditional values, driven by a burning drive to prove themselves, seeking for an area in which to do preferably an area in which they can gain power, and preferably, also in which in some symbolic way they can vent their rage at the elites who caused their troubles. The fact that the disparaging group cited above was traditional is one of the reasons why the disparaging group rejected traditional values and turned to innovation.[16]

A sociological theory of entrepreneurial supply was developed by Thomas Cochran. He starts with the premise that fundamental problems of economic development are noneconomic and hence he emphasised cultural values, role expectations and social sanctions as the key elements that determine the supply of entrepreneurs. According to him an entrepreneur is neither a super normal individual nor a deviant person but represents a society's modal personality. Hence the individual's performance as an entrepreneur will be influenced by their own attitude towards their occupation, the whole expectations held by sanctioning groups and the operational requirements of the job. The former two elements are determined largely by the society's values while the last element will be influenced by changes over time in such exogenous variable as population, technology, consumer demand or merely cumulative institutional drift.[17]

According to Frank Young the individual level entrepreneurial characteristics are interpreted as "under side" of a group level pattern. Instead of looking at individual, according to young, one must find clusters; ethnic communities, occupational groups or politically oriented factions. The chief aspects of this group definition of entrepreneurship is that the entrepreneur typically does not work single handed. He is simply the most visible member from an economic point of view of what is typically the cluster of families whose activities are mutually reinforcing and coordinated by a coherent outlook on the world.[18]

John H. Kunkel's behavioural model starts with the premise that man's internal state is beyond the scope of presently available means of measurements and objective analyses, and knowledge of it is largely unnecessary for the explanation and prediction of the behaviour. Hence the model is concerned instead with the overtly expressed activities of individual and their relations to the previously and presently surrounding social structure and physical conditions. According to this behavioural model change means activities that need not be concerned with altering values; one need to change only certain elements of the operant conditioning context of which all men at all times are an integral part.[19]

David C. McClelland wanted to find the internal factors, that is human values and motives that lead men to exploit opportunities, or what he called need for achievement, that is a desire to do well, not so much for the sake of social recognitions of prestige, but for the sake of an inner feeling of personal accomplishment. It is this motive of n- achievement that guides the actions of entrepreneur, people with high - n-achievements behave in an entrepreneurial way. According to him the entrepreneurs display the following characteristics:

(i) They do not work harder at routine works;

(ii) They avoid gambling situations because in such cases winning will only be due to luck and such winning does not give any sense of personal accomplishment; they want the outcome of their activities to depend on their own skill.

(iii) They show interest in finding out results of their decisions. For instant growth in sales, output or profit margin and such other economic indicators can be used to judge the effectiveness of entrepreneurial decisions.

(iv) They prefer to work hard at tasks that involve a real challenge which imply only a moderate risk.[20]

The n-achievement approach suggests promotion of achievement oriented ways of thinking to foster economic development in developing countries.

Harbinson also makes certain observations on entrepreneurship as a factor in economic development. He found identification of entrepreneur with an individual person in the context of modern industry as unreasonable. He categorises the functions of modern entrepreneurial organisation in the following way:

(i) The undertaking or managing of risk and the handling of economic uncertainty;

(ii) Planning and innovation;

(iii) Coordination, administration and control; and

(iv) Routine supervision.

In a small enterprise these different functions will be performed by the same individual. Harbinson characterises all the persons who perform entrepreneurial functioning in a large organisation as managerial resources. For him orgnaisation is more than a summation of particular abilities of certain individuals. Organisation connotes a constellation of functions in a common undertaking.

Hence Harbinson derives a few tentative hypotheses on the basis of his experience over two years with approximately 75 enterprises in England, France, Germany, Italy, Belgium, Holland, Egypt, Saudi Arabia, Peru and USA. The propositions are as stated below:

(i) Large expenditure for equipment and machinery are likely to be unproductive unless there is a corresponding investment in organisation.

(ii) Organisation is probably a principal factor determining the productivity of labour, assuming that capital and natural resources are constant;

(iii) Because of non-economic factors which determine in part the behaviour of human beings as managerial resources, all organisations are probably inefficient in affecting the optimum combination of economic resources which is theoretically possible.[21]

An economic model of entrepreneurship had been propounded by Peter Kilby. Using output as proxy for entrepreneurship and rate of return on investments as surrogate for entrepreneur's wage, Kilby shows the various possible shifts in supply and demand functions pertaining to entrepreneurship. The supply schedule is a function of socio-psychological variables and to some extent the past amount of entrepreneurial training. The derived demand for entrepreneurial services at any point in time is a function of the price of all cooperating factors of production, the stock of known or transferable technology, the level of managerial organisation and consumer's income. Given a favorable economic setting, the main function of enterprise is to make decisions under uncertainty. This model neglects the supply side of entrepreneurship and focuses on the demand side.

This model explains the lack of vigorous entrepreneurship in terms of various product and factor markets imperfections and inappropriate government policies, abrupt political changes etc. Thus diagnosis of a poor entrepreneurial performance makes economist suggest remedies like appropriate monetary, fiscal and trade policies, removal of market imperfections provision of inputs and technical assistance to industry.[22]

Kilby's model only highlights the environmental economic variables present on the demand side of the market for entrepreneurship. But the main drawback of Kilby's formulation is that it virtually assumes away, the supply side. The problem of entrepreneurship in developing economies like India is one of supply of entrepreneurship rather than demand for it. For this economists have to draw from socio-psychological theory. Also in view of the inter-disciplinary nature of the subject of entrepreneurship, the search for purely economic formulation is neither possible nor desirable. But it is necessary to identify as far as possible in a given context the major variables which influence entrepreneurial supply and its performance. Further an economic analysis of entrepreneurial performance would provide insights about entrepreneurial attitudes and motivation.

Lagan views entrepreneurship from a different angle. In his own words "Entrepreneurship is the process whereby people, money, market, production facility and knowledge are brought together to create a commercial enterprise which did not exist before". This is in Weberian tradition, according to which the entrepreneur is the ultimate source of authority in an organisation. However the contribution of these to the understanding of the concept of entrepreneurship is not substantial, because they have not tried to focus on the critical function of the entrepreneur, so the concept remains elusive. It is generally felt that entrepreneurship research has been staved by the lack of agreed definition of the context. There is no commonly accepted paradigm, and hence large sample studies across industries, locations and types of enterprise are not forthcoming. These problems are further complicated by the multitude of patterns identified in successful entrepreneurship leading to a clear need once again to begin from the first principles of classification.[23]

If we group all the theories of entrepreneurship, the role of the entrepreneur has been stressed to a higher degree by the psychological theories, followed by cultural theories, sociological theories and economic theories. If the role of environment is considered in the theories of entrepreneurship, there is a reversal of the above order. Hence there are in this group various intergroup relations that are complex and transgress the artificial boundaries unopposed. For instant economic theories, as adumbrated above, hold that entrepreneurship springs from the disequilibrium between demand and supply. If the cause of disequilibrium is attributed to changes in aggregate demand or aggregate supply, or to the developmental stage of the economy attained through maturation or through revolution and institutional change, then the role of individual entrepreneur in the process is minimal. However, if the disequilibrium is assumed to be caused by innovations made by the entrepreneur, then the strategic choice role is far greater than that of the environment.[24] It is also paradoxical that the psychological theories which are placed at the other end of the continuum speak their explanation in sociological and cultural events, on which the individual has very little control. McClelland, for instance proposes that achievement motive is the crucial cause of entrepreneurial behaviour, and stresses the origin of the motive to child-rearing practices based on religious ideology characterised by the protestant ethics. On the other hand the sociological theory proposed by Lagan does not dispense with the entrepreneurial individual; it states that such individuals emerge in community that have in the past experienced 'status drawal' or displacement. Each of these models seems to be relevant in its own way; environmental determinism may explain the macro level differences in entrepreneurship while strategic choice may explain the micro level differences between individuals within an economic system. Ideally the researcher should adopt a multifactor approach and recognise the constellation of forces acting upon the entrepreneur, rather than search only for a factor that could account for entrepreneurial behaviour. But at a particular point in time, it is the individual action, that is the strategic choice that would seem determine entrepreneurship. For this reason the focus of many studies for entrepreneurship has been the individual and his traits.

Entrepreneurship research has often been criticized for not having a research Paradigm one Paradigm is the strategic choice model, while the other model is called as the population - ecology model or environmental determinism model. The strategic choice model of organizational birth and deaths holds that entrepreneurial success depends primarily on the appropriateness of the individual's strategies rather than on the favourableness of the environment. The individual is capable of identifying opportunities, assembling resources and of developing appropriate strategies for ensuring the survival and growth of his venture. It is a process of constant adaptation to, and sometimes of manipulation and control of the environment through strategic choices. The population ecology model, on the other hand, minimizes the role of entrepreneur and holds that the survival of the organizations depends on the degree to which they are compatible with the environment.

Hannan and Freeman who first proposed this model 'felt that management theories generally over-emphasized the organisation's capacity to adopt to changes in their environment. They argued that the most dominant characteristic of organisations is inertia and so the basic process of organisations relationship with the environment is selection, not adaptation. This implies that organizational forms that happen to be compatible with the changed environment survive and grow and the non-compatible ones are selected out. The major features of the two models can be shown in the table given below.[25]

A Comparison between the Major Features of

Strategic Choice Model	Population Ecology Model
1. Acts of the entrepreneur are primarily volitional	1. Acts of the entrepreneur are primarily deterministic
2. The entrepreneur makes strategic choices to secure the best transactions with the environment	2. The entrepreneur's choices are predicted and moulded by the environment.
3. The environment is a pool of resources which the entrepreneur selects and acquires to establish his ventures.	3. The environment is a set of influences which selectively permit some ventures to survive.
4. The entrepreneur masters fate and makes strategic choices to minimize threats and exploit opportunities	4. The entrepreneur is a creature of the environment and an instrument of economic development.

Much of entrepreneurship research has implicitly assumed a strategic adaptation perspective and studies which focus on the role of the entrepreneurial individual in new venture creation subscribe to the often unstated assumptions of the strategic choice model. It is observed that entrepreneurs perform often in spite of the environment and are even capable of manipulating the environment some times and or converting the environmental constraints into opportunities.[26]

Proponents of Environmental determinism have their logic and some empirical evidence to suggest that organizations are trapped into their own inertia and get selected out by the environment. Another important reason for the apparent neglect of environment in entrepreneurship studies seems to be the fact that the impact of environmental factors depends partly on the individual's perceptions of the environment rather than on the objective reality. In the organizational context it was argued by some writers that it is the perceptions of uncertainty rather than the actual uncertainty that affect decision making and strategy formulation. It had also been pointed out that the ordinary organisations are unable to find a niche for themselves and hence blamed the environment, the innovative ones are able to gainfully exploit the limited opportunities provided by the environment. Thus perceptual differences make innovations possible even in environments that appear to be constraining and unfavourable to the general population. There are several cases of innovative entrepreneurs who have converted constraints into opportunities. For example, one of the largest and the most successful textile companies in India had its start-up during a period when the textile industry in the country was facing a particularly unfavourable environment. Such cases on the theories of perception seems to support the position that innovation is more a function of the individual strategic choices than that of environmental influences.[27]

Despite the perceptual difference there seems to be some kind of an agreement on the issue of what constitutes a favourable or conducive environment for entrepreneurial activities. A conducive environment is often understood as one in which resources are easily available, competition especially from abroad is restricted and political administration is benign with regard to infrastructure development, licencing, taxation, grants and subsidies, facilities for cheap credit, marketing facilities, training and extension services and nursing and rehabilitation of sick units. The emphasis is on the task environment and not on the general environment. The task environment consists of factors that have a specific impact on business activities such as:

(a) Customers including both distributors and users;

(b) Suppliers of materials, labour, capital and work space;

(c) Competitors for markets and resources and;

(d) Regulatory groups including governmental agencies, unions and interfirm associations, whereas the general environment consists of the economic, legal-political, socio-cultural and educational aspects. It has been observed that changes in the task environment affect only the entry of the innovative person into a particular field. They do not help the making of the innovative person; rather they provide or withdraw the opportunity for him to exercise his innovativeness in a particular domain of activity.[28]

Entrepreneurship Development Programmes

While the favourableness of the task environment is more an incentive to the imitator than to the innovator, changes in the general, especially the educational, environment are likely to influence the supply. It is in this context one has to understand the entrepreneurial development programmes. The entrepreneurship development is a key to achieve overall economic development through higher level of industrial activity. Entrepreneurship development programme is designed to help a person in strengthening and fulfilling his entrepreneurial motive and in acquiring skills and capabilities necessary for playing with entrepreneurial role effectively. Towards this end it is necessary to promote his understanding of motives, motivation pattern, their impact on behaviour and entrepreneurial value. A programme which seeks to do this can qualify to be called as a programmer. A number of programmes which aim at providing informational or managerial inputs or focus on invitation of a project. But even though all the inputs are required by a new entrepreneurial, the programme not touching entrepreneur motivation and behaviour cannot be called an EDP though EDP has been recognised as an effective human resource development tool. Many a times there are very many expectations from a single programme, like removing unemployment , enhancing industrial development, promoting small scale industries, developing industrially underdeveloped regions.

EDP is primarily meant for developing those first generation entrepreneurs who on their own cannot become successful entrepreneurs. It covers three major variables: location, target group and enterprise. Any of these can become the focus or starting point for initiating and implementing an EDP. The remaining two then will follow by making proper synthesis with the first. As for example, if the objective is to promote women entrepreneurs, suitable location and proper entrepreneurial activities must match or if the objective, is to develop North East region. Methodology for selection of the prospective entrepreneurs as well as support services after the training have a significant impact on the success of the entrepreneur development programme.[29]

These programmes broadly envisage a three tiered approach, developing achievement motivation and sharpening of entrepreneurial traits and behaviour, project planning and development and guidance on industrial opportunities, incentives and facilities and rules and regulations, and developing managerial and operational capabilities. Various techniques and approaches have been developed and adopted to achieve these objectives keeping in view the target groups and or to target areas.

Past experience has shown that industrial promotion by provision of facilities, technical assistance, management training, consultancy, industrial information and other services alone are not sufficient to develop entrepreneur. Hence the EDP package was launched over the years, the EDPs have become a vital strategy for harnessing the vast untapped human skills, to channelise them into accelerating industrialisation in general and growth of the small scale sector in particular.[30]

In line with the national programme for the promotion and development of small and medium industries in the countryside, the Industrial Service Institute (ISI) under the Department of Industrial Promotion (DIP) launched the EDP to give substance to the government's policies of stimulation of economic growth, dispersing industries to rural areas and promoting the processing of local raw materials. The EDP was considered a part of the industrial development policy which was articulated in the Five year national economic and social development plan.

Entrepreneurship Development Programme (EDP) in India has many objectives. The expert group constituted by the NIESBUD accepted that it must be able to help selected entrepreneurs to:[31]

(1) Develop and strengthen their entrepreneurial quality/motivation;

(2) Analyse environment related to small industry and small business;

(3) Select project/product;

(4) Formulate projects;

(5) Understand the process and procedure of setting up of small enterprise;

(6) Know and influence the source of help/support needed for launching the enterprise;

(7) Acquire the basic management skills;

(8) Know the pros and cons of being an entrepreneur; and

(9) Acquaint and appreciate the needed social responsibility/entrepreneurial disciplines.

Further some of the other important objectives of entrepreneurial training are:

i) To let the entrepreneur set or reset the objectives of his business and work individually and along with his group for their realisation.

ii) To prepare him for accepting totally unforeseen risks of business after such training.

iii) To enable him to take strategic decisions

iv) To enable him to build an integrated team to fulfil the demands of tomorrow.

v) To communicate fast, clearly and effectively

vi) To develop a broad vision to see the business as a whole and to integrate his function with it.

vii) To enable him to relate his product and industry to the total environment, to find what is significant in it and to take it into account in his decisions and actions.

viii) To enable him to cope with and coordinate all relevant paper work, most of which is statutorily obligatory.

ix) To make him accept industrial democracy, that is, accepting workers as partners in enterprise; and

x) To strengthen his integrity, honesty, and compliance with law, the key to success in the long run.

The basic features of Entrepreneurship Development Programme has gone through several modifications overtime as:

a) Identification and careful selection of entrepreneurs for training;

b) Developing the entrepreneurial capabilities of the trainee;

c) Equipping the trainee with the basic managerial understanding and strategies;

d) Ensuring a viable industrial project for each potential entrepreneur;

e) Helping him to secure the necessary financial, infrastructural and related assistance; and

f) Training cost is highly subsidised and only token fee is charged. A deposit is, however, taken to ensure commitment of participants.[32]

With the opening up of the Indian economy by virtue of global changes and also globalisation of markets entrepreneurship development needs a fresh outlook. It has been recognised that entrepreneurship development, particularly for micro, tiny and small industries had taken a deep root as a movement in all over country and the country has considerable expertise to share for the benefit for not only our own citizens but even for other developing countries of world. Hence a fresh look is needed at the strategies for gearing up our youth for entrepreneurial career, especially regarding the methodology of developing entrepreneurs is in our country.

The future entrepreneur of this new millennium has to face considerable challenges, severe competition not only from the national angle but also from the global angle. This is more so in the case of such areas like consumer products which till now had some protection. The future entrepreneur, hence has to be prepared through training and exposure for planning and launching an enterprise keeping in mind the following:[33]

a) Technology and scope for modernization.
b) Quality including ISO- 90,00 requirements
c) Consumer satisfaction / customer service
d) Energy conservation
e) Pollution / environmental aspects
f) Cost of production
g) Competition from both national and international angles.

The EDP models will therefore have to be developed taking these aspects into consideration. Unlike the past, today the openings are many to talented youth who can take certain amount of risk in planning entrepreneurship as a career either through manufacturing/processing industry or through servicing or business enterprises which support these activities. For instance some new opportunities are emerging in processing industries like mushroom processing or through demands. Other areas are floriculture or software export or sweet meats exports which have no relevance a decade ago. With the emphasis now given to clean environment and clean technology, there will be many more opportune futures which entrepreneurship development need.

During the 8th Plan Period (1995-2002) the Government of India has taken some initivatives for the entrepreneurship developemnt through the department of small industry. For the first time separate policy measures for the growth and development of village and small scale industries was announced during August 1991. These policy measures have spelt out clearly many issues related to HRD for SSI sector including entrepreneurship development. They are as follows:

i) Govt will continue to support the first generation entrepreneur through training and will support their efforts. A large number of EDP trainers and motivators will be trained to significantly expand the EDP. Industry associations would also be encouraged to involve and participate in this venture effectively;

ii) Topics on EDP would be integrated in to the curricula of vocational and other degree level courses;

iii) Women entrepreneurs will receive support through special training programmes.

iv) Additional employment opportunities would be generated through training of multi-disciplinary "Bare Foot" managers to suit the special requirements of SSI sector.

Towards implementation of these policy measures, the following plan programmes have been introduced:

a) Supporting existing EDP institutions for infrastructural development leading to improvement in training methodology and contents;

b) Evaluation of ongoing EDP activities;

c) Developing a cadre of management assistants suitable for small scale entrepreneurs;

d) Promoting entrepreneurship amongst women, weaker sections of the society, organising special skill related and process oriented EDPs which are relevant to Micro and Tiny enterprises.

A National Entrepreneurship Development Board has also been constituted in the department of SSI and A and RI , one recent development that has taken place with respect to developing trade related EDPs for women. These EDPs are expected to develop women entrepreneurs in all aspects and gear them up to take up exports in a big way either individually or in groups. It is also felt that in view of a good number of clusters which are operated by women existing in different parts of India. Institutions like IED and CEDS will have to look at this important target group and work out the EDP methodology/ strategy. In such a programme, in addition to class room type of training, linkages will have to be developed towards developing designs, improved manufacturing techniques, upgrading the skills of the workers and supervisors, packaging, marketing, etc.

Growth of the SSI required creation and fostering of entrepreneurship on a mass scale. However in tradition bound societies like India, with the rigid occupational and social structure the source of supply of entrepreneurship was limited to certain classes, communities and regions. This limited source of supply was grossly inadequate in view of the growing demand of entrepreneurs in the context of current phase of globalisation. Therefore the entrepreneurial based needs to be burdened by directing the non-traditional classes/areas also into the main stream of entrepreneurship.

This entrepreneurship developed among educated youth especially among technical personnel. This further accentuated and added a new dimension to the need of widening the entrepreneurial base. Hence the attempts at fostering entrepreneurship through training ventures.

In India many organisations are participating in the entrepreneurship development programme.

The permanent institutions fostering entrepreneurship development in India are as given here under: SIDO, SIST, DIC, NSIC, SSIC, SDI, SFC, Banks, SIETI, CITD, ISI, Export Promotion Council and STC.

The interrelation among the various institutions is as shown in Figure 1[34]:

The institutions fostering entrepreneurial development are as follows:

1) The Small Industries Development Organisations (SIDO)
2) National Small Industries Corporation (NSIC)

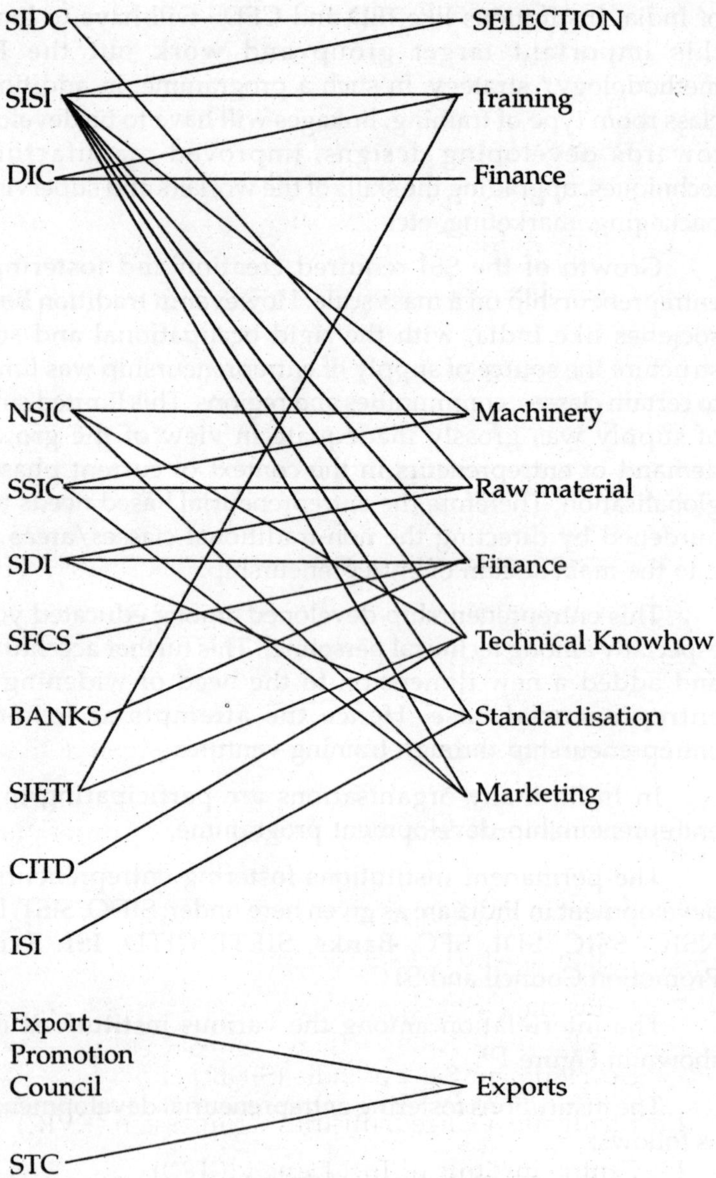

Fig 1: Institutions Assisting Entrepreneurs in Small Industries.

3) Directorates of Industries of state government.
4) State Small Industries Corporation (SSIC)
5) Small Industry Extension Training Institute (SIET)
6) Small Scale Industries Board (SSIB)
7) Indian Investment Centre (IIC)
8) Bureau of Industrial Costs and Prices (BICP)
9) Controller of General Patents, Designs and Trade Marks.
10) Export Promotion Councils (EPC)
11) Commodity Boards (CB)
12) Export Houses (EHS)
13) Indian Institute of Packaging (IIP)
14) Expert Inspection Council (EIC)
15) Indian Council of Arbitration (ICA)
16) Jute Corporation of India (JCI)
17) The State Trading Corporation of India (STC)
18) The Minerals & Metals Trading Corporation of India (MMTC).
19) The National Industrial Development Corporation (NIDC).
20) National Productivity Council (NPC)
21) Indian Bureau of Standards (IBS)
22) Industrial Development Bank of India (IDBI) and its newly subsidiary The Small Industrious Development Bank of India (SIDBI).
23) Khadi and Village Industries Commission (KVIC)
24) Central Institute of Tool Design (CITD)
25) District Industries Centres (DIC)

26) The Institute for Design for Electrical Measuring Increments (IDEMI)

27) National Institute for Small Industry Extension Training (NISIET)

28) National Institute for Entrepreneurship and Small Business Development (NIESBUD)

29) National Institute of Design (NID)

30) The World Bank (WB)

31) Entrepreneurship Development Institute of India (EDII)

32) National Entrepreneurship Development Board (NEDB)

33) National Science & Technology Entrepreneurship Developemnt Board (NSTEDB)

34) National Research Development Corporation & National Research Laboratories of CSIR

35) Commodity Board in 8 areas of Coffee, tea, coir, handicrafts, handlooms, silks, rubber and cardamom.

36) Chamber of Commerce & Industry Association of Trade and Industry like The Federation of Association of Small Industries of India, National Association of Young entrepreneurs (NAYE)

37) Export Processing Zones (EPZ).

38) Industrial Finance Corporation of India (IFCI)

39) Industrial Credit Investment Corporation of India (ICICI).

40) Risk Capital and Technology Finance Corporation of India (RCTC).

41) Industrial Reconstruction Bank of India (IRBI).

42) The Investor Promotion Board.

43) Small Industries Development Corporation (SIDC)

44) Small Industry Service Institutes (SISI)

45) Industries Infrastructure Corporation (IIC)

46) State Financial Corporations (SFCs)

47) Technical Consultancy Organisation (TCO).

48) Entrepreneurship Developemnt Cells (EDCs)

49) Science & Technology Entrepreneurship Parks (STEPS)

50) Commercial Banks.[35]

The incentives and facilities for development of small scale industries had been delineated.

Fresh Incentives

1) Excise concession available for Board registered and unregistered units upgraded scale depending upon turnover up to Rs 3,00,000/-.

2) Quality certification scheme launched to improve SI product Quality. Financial support to acquire ISO 9000.

3) Seven point Action plan initiated to improve credit flow to SSI sector, Fifty-one sepcialized SSI branches opened.

4) Scope of National Equity Fund scheme enlarged over the whole country except metropolitan areas to support expansion, modernisation and technology upgradation.

5) Technology Developemnt and Moderation Fund scheme launched for modernisation and adoption of improved and updated technology.

6) A scheme for creation of Technology Development Fund in the states launched with the involvement of state government and Industry Association.

Credit Policies

* Priority sector lending.
* 40% of advance to SSI sector reserved for Tiny sector and village and cottage industries.
* Concessional/Fixed rates of interest for loans up to Rs. 2 Lakhs (2 slabs)
* Single window scheme of SIDBI for project outlays up to Rs. 50 Lakhs.

Other Incentives

* Reservation of products for exclusive manufacture (836 products at present)
* Purchase and price preference.
* Infrastructure support to entrepreneurship Development Institutes to augment their training capacities.
* Entrepreneurship Development Institute set up in Guwahati, Assam for improving the entrepreneurial base for the North Eastern Region.
* Joint programme with the State Bank of India and Small Industries Development Bank of India for modernization and technology upgradation of industry clusters.
* Assistance to industrial associations voluntary agencies to set up testing centres.
* Special programmes on vendor development, quality awareness and pollution control.[36]

Models of Entrepreneurship Development

Some methods of entrepreneurship developemnt in India have been experimented. Among these the nature of 5 models will be discussed here.

a) SIET model [37]

SIET Institute, Hyderabad in collaboration with D.C. McClelland of Harvard University conducted certain experiments called Kakinada Experiment to verify the theory of achievement motivation in developing entrepreneurship. Six Training experiments each of two weeks duration were conducted during 1964-1965 with 52 participants from Kakinada (Andhra Pradesh), 26 participants from Vellore (Tamil Nadu) who had already set up SSI units. This is like a before-after experiment where after the completion of the training, performance comparison of trainees with control group an equal number of untrained entrepreneurs., showed significant improvement in entrepreneurial performance of trainees.

Another experiment in training programme was conducted of 12 weeks duration for unemployed engineering graduates by SIET in 1970. The objectives of this programme were to enable the trainees to take up entrepreneurship, to impart skills in selecting a product, planning and setting up of a unit and to impart managerial skills. A follow up study in 1973 by SIET Faculty had revealed that out of 155 potential entrepreneurs trained, about one half had either set up or in the process of setting up of their units. SIET launched training programmes for self employed youth in other states like J&K in 1972, for Assam in 1974 and also for Karnataka. Only 17 out of 95 trainees could set up their enterprises and among these in the same state all the 16 trainees started their enterprises with in a year.

Though these experiments were encouraging, another follow up study by SIET faculty in 1974 disclosed that the trained entrepreneurs faced problems like procuring adequate raw material, inadequate or delayed financial assistance, inability to lend after-sales-service and long and large over dues from the debtors.

The above problems faced by entrepreneurs emphasised the fact that it is not enough to motivate the trainees to set up enterprises.

1. Entrepreneurial education
2. Publicity on entrepreneurial opportunities.
3. Identification of potential entrepreneurs.
4. Motivational training to new entrepreneurs.
5. Guidance in selecting products and preparing project reports.
6. Providing techno-economic information and product profile
7. Evolving new products and process.
8. Local agencies with trained personnel for counseling and promotion
9. Creating entrepreneurial forums.

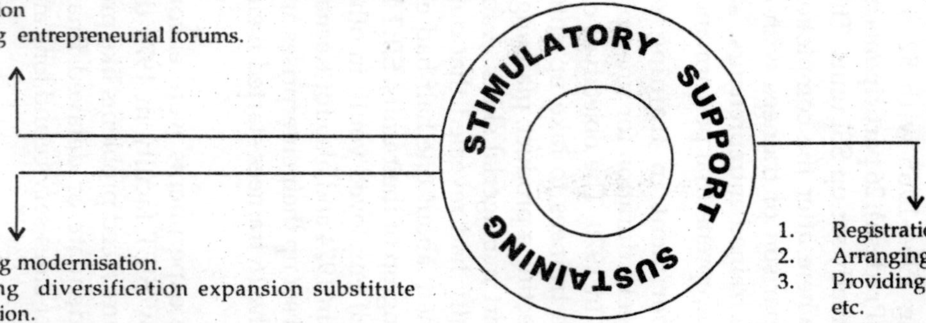

1. Assisting modernisation.
2. Assisting diversification expansion substitute production.
3. Additional financing for full capacity utilisation
4. Deferring repayment interest.
5. Diagnostic industrial extension / consultancy source
6. Production units legislation polic change
7. Production reservation creating new avenue for marketing
8. Quality testing and improving services.
9. Need based common in facilities centre.

1. Registration of the unit
2. Arranging finance
3. Providing land, shed, power, water etc.
4. Guidance for obtaining machinery.
5. Supply of scarce raw materials.
6. Getting licenses
7. Providing common facilities.
8. Tax relief or other subsidy
9. Offering management consultancy.
10. Marketing assistance.
11. Providing information.

Figure 2.2 SIET Model

In order to realise the objectives of entrepreneurship development, SIET evaluated an integrated model of EDP in 1974. The essence of this model is to coordinate and synchronise the functions of the supporting agency as shown in the Figure 1.

Among the activities that will generate motivation among potential entrepreneurs that can be called as stimulatory activities, the model included activities like education in business opportunities, identification of potential entrepreneur, motivating them by providing business and economic insights and managerial skills through training, helping entrepreneurs to think of new products for which demand exists and project feasibility report, making available techno-economic information, setting up local agencies with trained personnel for entrepreneurial counseling and motivation, creating forums for entrepreneurs to discuss a common problem.

The next type of activity or support activities that are intended to help entrepreneurs in setting up and commissioning the unit include activities like registration of a unit, arranging finance, provision of common facilities including land and building, consulting services, provision of scarce raw materials, tax relief concessions and marketing assistance.

The Third type of activities are sustaining activities that include continued association of all the supporting agencies to sustain and develop the enterprise. These include technology upgradation, expansion and diversification of production.

The SIET model can be represented in the form of circular activity. The cycle shows that stipulatory activity of entrepreneurship development under favourable conditions lends to supporting activities crystalising into setting up of enterprises. Once the enterprises pickup, some of the supporting activities are needed for their sustenance and development. The same sequence used not be followed in practice as all the activities can be initiated simultaneously.

(b) Gujarat Model[38]

Gujarat Industrial Corporation launched the Technicians

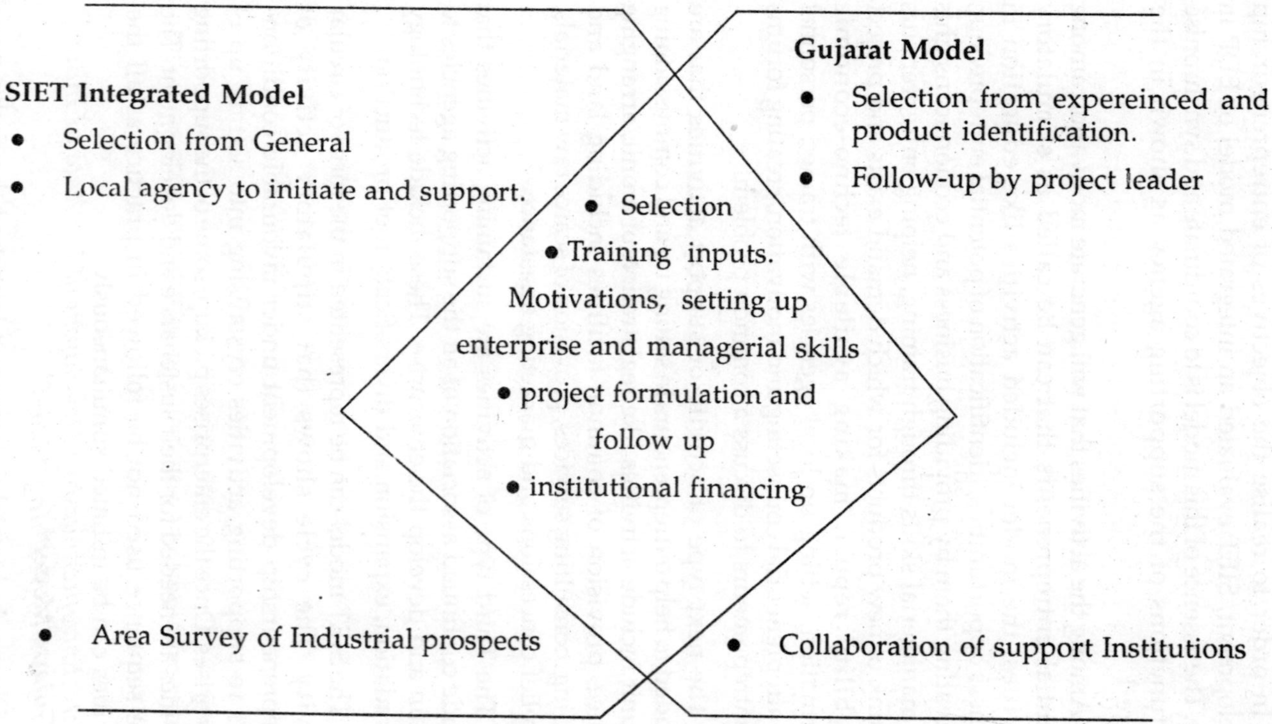

Figure 2.3 Integrated Model of SIET and Gujarat Models

Scheme in 1969 offering loan finance up to 100 per cent of the fixed assets, working capital margin and preliminary and pre-operative expenses to technically qualified or experienced persons who have viable projects. The scheme was later extended to non-technicians, especially employees with industrial experience, sales management or business graduate and new entrepreneur scheme (NES).

Need based financing and reliance on the entrepreneurs' capabilities and competencies rather than their financial position were the main criteria of financing under the scheme. Encouraged by the results of technicians' scheme, four corporations in Gujarat (GIIC, GITC, GSFC, and GSIC) jointly sponsored a programme for developing entrepreneurs in 1970, a three months training-cum development programme for technicians, traders, employees in private firms , sales men and professionals who have motivation and project plans. The Gujarat model has incorporated its EDP features like identifying potential entrepreneur, assisting the trainee entrepreneur to prepare viable project, developing entrepreneurial and managerial skills of training and providing them with financial and infrastructure facilities so that the new units are set up with in a shortest possible records. A comparison of SIET and Gujarat model is shown in the Figure 2.3.

The contrast between the two models shows that SIET model aims at electing potential entrepreneur from the general public whereas Gujarat model focuses on the experience. The SIET model assigns an important role to a local agency to initiate and support entrepreneurship, besides the survey of the industrial prospects as an important input. On the other hand in Gujarat model role of support institution is considered important. Thus both models highlight the significant role of support agencies. The training inputs are similar in both the models.

(c) *Entrepreneurship Development Institute of India (EDII) Training Model*[39]

Another model has been developed by EDII. According

to this institute model, the general stages of EDP may be broadly divided into three stages:

a) Pre-training

b) Training, and

c) Post-training.

Stage One: *Pre-Training*. In this stage the selection of local/centre and pre-training promotion work for creation of EDP awareness, identification and selections of potential entrepreneur, choosing training inputs as well as local and out side trainers and promising class room facilities and aids are the important aspects of this stage.

Stage Two: Training. The duration of the training varies from Two to Twelve weeks. The ideal duration would be a six weeks full-time programme and twelve weeks part-time programmes. The training inputs are spread over three phases as given below:

Phase	*Inputs*	*Objectives*
Phase -I	Behavioural inputs Business opportunity guidance.	To develop personality traits and self-confidence. To seize suitable business opportunity.
Phase - II	Information Technical inputs	To guide in the project formulation. To assist in drawing of projects plans.
Phase -III	Managerial inputs	To impart managerial skills for the operations of the unit.

On the basis of the target group, the trainer may select any combination of the following methods: Lecture, case studies, business , games, problem oriented exercises, syndicate methods, video films, group discussions presentations royal play, shop floor lectures and experiential learning. During these sessions, there may be four to six field visits and four - six days of input study. Another one to two weeks may be required to prepare the actual project reports on selected topics. Taking all these considerations into account, the total EDP training duration may be six to ten weeks.

Stage -3: Post-Training:

Post-training support involves:

a) Follow up on loan application for finance,

b) Provision of infrastructure such as land, sheds, power, water etc., and finally

c) Trouble shooting.

The need for sustained follow-up arises, partly for reasons of indecisiveness of some of the trainees and their low levels of motivation and the unanticipated response to the training from the support agencies. Thus the nature of follow-up supports include technical and financial guidance like preparing reports, filling loan application etc., and coordination with financial support institution. Support is also rendered for miscellaneous contingent problem arising out of the process of the implementation.

(d) Udai Pareek and Nadkarni Model[40]

Pareek and Nadkarni presented a role transformation model for the emergence of entrepreneurs. They have identified four sets of factors that influence entrepreneurship. They are : 1) individual; the society and family make individual internalize certain values and names which transform into an entrepreneur.

2. Socio-cultural Traditions: The entrepreneurs who are influenced by the society and family themselves generate socio cultural environemnt and traditions and influence others in more or less degree.

3. Socio-political Economic Policy: The policies of the govt and other financial institutions determine the opportunities available.

4. Support Systems: These includes financial and commercial institution research, trainee and consultancy services.

In this model, the role of social cultural factors is that of the initiator and intervening impetus is provided by support system including political and economic environment.

Table 2.1: Role Transformation Model

Stages	*Behavoiurs*
Phase I. Identity search:	
Identity crisis	Dissatisfaction with present identity.
Exploration	Looking-out for ways of reducing the dissatisfaction
Transitional stress	Apprehensions about the new identity
Search	Search for entrepreneurial alternative.
Deliberations	Weights pros and cons of each alternatives
Choice	Makes a tentative choice from the alternative
Phase II. Identity formation:	
Pre-enterprise	Collecting information on business preparation opportunities cand preparing project report.
Enterprising building	Setting up an enterprise
New Identity	Becoming an entrepreneur.
Phase III. Identity establishment:	
Enterprise management	Managing the enterprise
Role stress	Entrepreneurial stress and strain.
Identity integration	Identity with other entrepreneurs.
Linkage building	Establishes linkage with other entrepreneurs and support systems.

The role transformation model, as shown in the figure consists of two phases namely identity search and identity formation. The first phase involved the ending of old identity and searching for a new identity. It is in this phase that an entrepreneurial alternative is to be put in the mind of individual. The identity formation requires the intervention by support organisation.

(e) Ghaziabad Model[41]

The training and placement cell of the Govt. Polytechnic Ghaziabad analyzed the existing design of the entrepreneurship development programmes. The cell prepared a more refined and effective model for the organization of the programmes. The faculty of the polytechnic found that their programmes could not motivate the students to start their own enterprise after attending entrepreneurship development programmes. Therefore the training and placement cell prepared a refined model for the unemployed technical persons. The main points for the model are:

- Knowledge of entrepreneurship must be given through curriculum,
- In final year, structured training must be given through awareness camp,
- Expert lectures by officials from DICs, banks, financial agencies and other management experts on entrepreneurship,
- Get-together with established entrepreneurs, so that the participants have an idea of proven success stories,
- After completion of camp, a team comprising officials from DIC, UPSFC, bank, faculty members and established entrepreneurs must evaluate the participants and select the talented ones,
- The selected participants must be given stipend until he starts earning through his own enterprise,
- The team members must visit and counsel the participants on various problems during the establishment period,

- After establishment, the team members must provide follow-up support from time to time, until they satisfy that participant has developed into a successful entrepreneur, and
- The success story can become real motivation to others to follow.

The above model will definitely help in making entrepreneurship development programmes meaningful. They will help in turning the attention of youth towards self-employment, which in turn will be useful in decreasing the unemployment scenario to some extent.

Apart from the above specific models that have been experimented, it is estimated that EDP work is being undertaken by over forty different agencies all over the country. Taking clues from the Gujarat model of the EDP, various branches and offices of State Bank of India throughout the country have conducted programmes especially for educated unemployed in industrially backward districts. The other agencies engaged in EDP work may be grouped as follows:

i) 15 Small Industries Service Institutes (SISIs) set up by the Government of India. They conduct programmes primarily for fresh engineers, technical diploma holders and unemployed science graduates.

ii) 16 Technical Consultancy Organisations (TCOs) jointly sponsored by all India financial institutions. Industrial Development Bank of India (IDBI), Industrial Credit and Investment Corporation of India Limited (ICICI) and Industrial Finance Corporation of India (IFCI), along with state level financial institutions. TCO programmes for entrepreneurship development are meant for young graduates, educated unemployed, and in some cases, experienced employees, traders and women.

iii) Some 10 to 12 other agencies such as nationalised banks (other than SBI), management Institutes and voluntary organisations, universities and colleges also are now beginning to start EDPs by way of a few elective papers as part of their regular course of study.

With such a burgeoning of EDP activities, it was felt that the time was ripe for the emergence of some apex, all India institution to help and guide the next phase of consolidation and development of EDP work in the country.[42]

Studies on Entrepreneurship and EDP

A review of the studies on entrepreneurship and EDP highlight the traits among entrepreneurs as well as a social pattern. The main conclusions of some of the earlier studies on entrepreneurship is summarised here[43]:

1) The studies by Gadgil and Medhora come to the conclusion that the caste system and its obligations tend to reduce occupational mobility, technical change, and innovation, which go against the social and religious prescriptions. It is necessary to mention in this connection that the studies are related to an earlier period of the industrialization of the country.

2) Hazlehurst in his study notes that refugee entrepreneurs tend to be more innovative than local entrepreneurs.

3) On the basis of the social origins (caste or social community to which entrepreneurs belong) of the sample entrepreneurs, Berna concludes that in explaining entrepreneurial activity economic factors such as access to capital, possession of business experience and technical knowledge are more important than sociological factors such as caste, attachment to traditional activities, and approval or disapproval of the social group to which a potential entrepreneur belongs.

4) Hazlehurst's study reveals that in many cases the extended family is the limit of entrepreneurship,

supplying managerial and financial resources needed for business and industrial operations.

5) Singh's study discloses that the public enterprises are characterised by low profit and savings rates which may be partly due to lack of entrepreneurial skills in the public sector.

6) In Berna's sample of entrepreneurs, 12 out of 52 were graduate engineers which may be taken as indicative of the fact that technocrats may constitute a major source of entrepreneurial supply.

7) The political and socio-economic changes that are taking place in the country during the post-independence period might have reduced the rigidity of the caste system and has helped occupational mobility.

In the earlier period prior to 1980 a number of studies were conducted on entrepreneurship but after 1980 the number of studies proliferated on different aspects of entrepreneurship. Among the researchers who conducted field studies, one study of 54 manufacturing units conducted by Nasziger in the Visakhapatnam city of Andhra Pradesh shows that the economic status of the father was closely related to entrepreneurial success.

V. Lakshmana Rao studied 51 entrepreneurs in two coastal districts of Andhra Pradesh and found that a majority of entrepreneurs were natives and belonged to upper castes having previous experience in the same field. However their level of education and economic status were low.

B.E.V.V.N. Murthy studied the socio-economic profiles, ambitions, influencing factors of entrepreneurs in two selected towns of Andhra Pradesh and observed the loosening of the hold of caste on occupations. As a result, enterprising farmers and artisans were turning to occupations other than caste occupations. The facilitating factors are encouragement by friends/relatives/family members, contacts with business people, and success stories of entrepreneurs, previous experience and property inherited/acquired.[44]

N.P. Singh and Rita Sengupta in their survey of 45 potential women entrepreneurs observed that 1. married women were more attracted towards entrepreneurship due to getting male help and support; 2. the need for achievement was moderate; and 3. Majority of them were from middle income group.

Pannalal studied a sample of industrial estates in Andhra Pradesh. His inferences were that entrepreneurs were mostly middle aged, that is they are in the age group of 31-40 years. Secondly parents background had a catalytic role, especially among those whose parents belonged to industry, trade and contract works.

Thirdly the organisational setup was mostly single proprietorships, which was not only popular but also successful and the other common form was partnership. As regards the industries that were more successful, engineering industries were thriving in industrial estates, constituting 62 per cent of the sample.[45]

K. Madhu Murthy conducted a study of 80 entrepreneurs from Warangal, Visakhapatnam and Hyderabad. He found that entrepreneurs supply is mostly from those who belong to agricultural and business families. They are relatively young, that is in between 25-30 years and graduates. Among these graduates engineering graduates had some earlier experience before they had set up their establishments. The motivational factors for choosing entrepreneurial career are desire for independent life, personal fame innovation and encouragement by several agencies.[46]

Some studies have highlighted the effectiveness of EDPs. P.N. Singh provided an overview of Entrepreneurship development in India, focussing on factors considered to be important for nurturing entrepreneurship. P. Asthana reviewed the experiences of EDPs in India and abroad. The author, while suggesting a model programme raised some important issues regarding (a) structure and composition of EDPs, (b) Areas of operations (c) Fixing of priorities (d) Follow-up (e) spatial dispersal of EDPs (f) Training of trainers and (g) Pattern and financing new ventures[47].

V.G. Patel under a World Bank research project studied the three Gujarat innovations, (i) The technicians and new entrepreneurs scheme of finance (TSNES) (ii) Entrepreneurship development programme (EDP) & iii) The sheds construction programme for industrial infrastructure, to assess the effectiveness of such innovative policies and programmes in new entrepreneurship formation. The conclusions of the study are (i) programmes are effective and accelerating the development of small scale industries; (ii) potential industrial entrepreneurship is lying latent in a variety of castes, communities and occupational groups, (iii) success in the ventures is the result of enterprise and competence rather than financial position of the entrepreneur; and (iv) EDPs can address those with inadequate entrepreneurial and managerial capacities and industrial information and self-confidence.

Ravi K. Zutshi discussed the need to mould entrepreneurs who are better equipped to create hitech enterprises. In order to nurture entrepreneurship among persons with science and technical education, the author suggested a programme package consisting of entrepreneurial awareness, skill developemnt, prototype design and project work and confidence building.[48]

Nagendra P. Singh attempted at redefining the interrelated facets of EDP and explained the methodology of entrepreneurship development, process and design. The author reviewed the Indian experiences and examined several alternatives for initiating EDP for different target groups.[49]

Some of the problems faced by entrepreneurs have been discussed by some authors. Ajit Kanitkar advocated the adoption of extension approach by the support systems. He found that the low success rate of entrepreneurship training programme was to be attributed to the unsympathetic and often hostile response of the the support system. Based on the experience of organizing two extension motivation programmes in the North Eastern states of India, he concluded that human component of the support system had to be sensitized to imfluence the external environment. V.G. Patel found that poor involvement of the institutions as also of the trainers, and the faulty selection of the geographical area and target group had contributed largely to the failures of EDPs. Desingu Setty had discussed the problems and prospects of promoting entrepreneurship in small industry and the author suggested suitable support systems for each class of problem. MMP Akhouri after examining the policies, programmes and progress made by SSI in ten Asian countries, highlighted the concept of integrated entrepreneurship development and its close linkages to the SSI development with the help of empirical evidence. He also highlighted the policy implementation gaps in Entrepreneurship development.[50]

The above research studies are related to the experiences of entrepreneurs organising mostly SSI units in different parts of the country. The experiences of entrepreneurs functioning in the state of Andhra Pradesh based on the various EDPs as well as research studies conducted by different authors will be presented in the next chapter.

NOTES

1. David H. Holt, *Entrepreneurship New Venture Creation*, Prentice Hall of India, New Delhi, 1998, p. 2.
2. *Ibid.*, p. 3.
3. *Ibid.*, p. 6.
4. Vasanth Desai, *Dynamics of Entrepreneurial Development and Management*, Himalaya Publishing House, Mumbai, 1999, pp. 16-17.
5. David H. Holt, *Entrepreneurship*, op. cit., p. 7.
6. *Ibid.*, p. 7.
7. *Ibid.*, p. 7.
8. *Ibid.*, pp. 8-9.

9. *Ibid.*, p. 11.
10. Vasanth Desai, *Dynamics of Entrepreneurial Development and Management*, op. cit., p. 53.
11. *Ibid.*, p. 55.
12. *Ibid.*, p. 58.
13. J.S. Saini, "Entrepreneurship and Economic Development" in J. Saini and S.K. Dhameja (Ed) *Entrepreneurship and Small Business*, Rawat Publication, Jaipur, 1998, p. 16.
14. V. Laxmana Rao, *Industrial Entrepreneurship in India*, Chug Publications, Allahabad, 1991, p. 40.
15. R. Venkatapathy, *Cognitive Self among First Generation Entrepreneurs and Second Generation Entrepreneurs*, SEDME, Vol. xviii; December, 1991, p. 16.
16. *Ibid.*, p. 50.
17. *Ibid.*, p. 52.
18. *Ibid.*, p. 53.
19. *Ibid.*, p. 54.
20. *Ibid.*, pp. 55-56.
21. *Ibid.*, pp. 57-58.
22. *Ibid.*, p. 61.
23. Matua J. Manimal, *Jobs for Social Transformation - Entrepreneurial Policies and Strategies the Innovator Choice*; Sage Pub, New Delhi, 1999.
24. *Ibid.*, p. 62.
25. Matua J. Manimala, *Entrepreneurship Theory at the Crossroads Paradigms and Praxis*, Wheeler & Co. Ltd., New Delhi, 1999, pp. 19-20.
26. *Ibid.*, p. 20.
27. *Ibid.*, pp. 21-22.
28. *Ibid.*, p. 22.
29. Vasanth Desai, *Dynamics*, op. cit., p. 134.
30. *Ibid.*, p. 136.
31. *Ibid.*, p. 137.

32. *Ibid.*, p. 139.
33. N.K.A. Rao, *Entrepreneurship Development*—2001 National Social Science Documentation Centre (ICSIR), New Delhi.
34. Vasant Desai, Institutions for Entrepreneurial Development, Vol.- II, Himalaya Publishing House, 1999, New Delhi, p. 27.
35. *Ibid.*, p. 27 and Government of India Economic Survey, 1995-96 p. 126.
36. Government of India Economic Survey, 1995-96, op. cit.
37. Kathayini, *A Study on Entrepreneurial Attitudes of Students*.
38. *Ibid.*, pp. 45-48.
39. *Ibid.*, pp.48-50.
40. *Ibid.*, pp.50-52.
41. Pankaz Sharma, 'Entrepreneurship Development' in J.S. Saini and K. Dhameja (ED): *Enrtrepreneurship and Small Business*, Rawat Publication, Jaipur, 1998, pp. 12-15.
42. R. Radha Krishnan, *An evaluation of Entrepreneurship development programmes in Tamil Nadu*, unpublished thesis, Kakatiya University, 1994, pp. 123-124.
43. V. Lakshmana Rao, *Industrial Entrepreneurship in India*, Chugh Publications, Allahabad, (India) 1986, pp. 73-75.
44. Kathayini, *A Study on Entrepreneurial Attitudes of Students*, pp. 70-71.
45. Ponnalal, Status of small scale enterprises in Industrial estates in Andhra Pradesh: A study, SEDME, volume 21, Number 4 December 1994, pp. 57-58.
46. Madhu Murthy, Some aspects of entrepreneurship development in developing economics with special reference to India, unpublished Ph.D Thesis submitted to K.U., Warangal, 1997.
47. Kathayini, *A Study of Entrepreneur Attitudes*, op. cit., p. 83.
48. *Ibid.*
49. *Ibid.*
50. *Ibid.*, pp. 87-88.

3

Entrepreneurship Development Programmes in Andhra Pradesh with Special Reference to Small Scale Industrial Sector

The utility of entrepreneurship development is reflected mainly in the growth of the SSI sector at the State level. Hence a brief review of the growth of SSI Sector in Andhra Pradesh has been attempted here.

Small Scale Industries form a significant part of Andhra Pradesh economy. This sector contributes around 6 per cent of gross state domestic product and employs about 2.5 lakh people. In keeping with the general policy towards the development of small scale sector and its policies to develop women and disadvantaged groups, entrepreneurship among these groups is being encouraged. Emphasis will be laid on identifying Industrial activity suitable to the area in which disadvantaged groups live and to the creation of infrastructure, augmentation of credit and capability building for these groups. This will include helping them to acquire technical and managerial skills through training programme.[1]

In the earlier plan special emphasis was laid on promoting small scale and labour intensive industries to provide greater employment opportunities particularly in rural areas. The approach adopted during the Seventh Plan, was to insure fair dispersal of industries reducing inequalities between regions.

Growth and Dispersal of Industries in Andhra Pradesh

In Andhra Pradesh the Commissioner of Industries is incharge of the execution of extension programmes in the field of industrial development with stress on promotion of small scale, village and cottage industries which contribute to employment generation and development in rural economy. The district industries centres established earlier in all the district headquarters are providing all services and support under single roof to prospective entrepreneurs to set up small industries in the rural areas. They further undertake several programmes like identifying and motivating the entrepreneurs through campaign, training artisans, assisting artisans and tiny units through grants, loans towards rural industrialisation. The Government of India was sharing 60 per cent of the expenditure incurred under establishment charges of DIC. The programme of DIC produced significant growth in the sector of village and small industries.

The SSI board and development commissioner (SI) looks after the policy framework as well as the promotion and development of SSI. In the context the office of the development commissioner, known as Small Industries Development Organisation(SSIO), prepares the estimates of the number SSI units, production, employment and exports.

At the all India level there were 0.42 million units in 1973-74 and their numbers increased to 3.01 million units by 1997-98. Their production was estimated as Rs. 72,000 millions at current prices in 1973-74 and it increased to Rs. 46,51,710 million in 1997-98, signifying a very high rate of increase in the value of production by small scale units (SSI). Employment provided by these units also signify a four fold increase in 1973-74. The SSI units were providing employment to 3.97 million, while this increased to 16.72 million in 1997-98. In 1973-74 these units were exporting rupees 3,930 million worth of goods, while in

1997-98 this value increased to Rs. 4,39,460 million.[2] Thus the SSI sector had been showing progress in the last three decades.

The Table 3.1 shows number of units, employment, investment and production of SI, in the state of Andhra Pradesh.

Table 3.1
Growth of SSI Sector in Andhra Pradesh

Year	*No. of Units*	*Employment*	*Fixed Investment (Rs. Million)*	*Production (Rs. Million)*
1987-88	39,210	276,127	6.258	NA
1988-89	48,547	361,256	7.307	NA
1989-90	56,490	414,976	7.925	NA
1990-91	63,848	471,541	8.817	NA
1991-92	71,554	538,991	9.926	NA
1992-93	77,755	580,445	11.480	NA
1993-94	83,367	626,807	13.052	NA
1994-95	87,802	667,706	14.902	NA
1995-96	91,909	701,512	16.810	NA
1996-97	96,879	739,422	18.917	NA
1997-98	101,814	789,421	21.889	NA

Source: SIDBI Report on SSI sector, p. 228.

The above table shows that the number of units in Andhra Pradesh has increased from 39,210 in 1987-88 to 1,01,814 units in 1997-98 indicating that there had been about 2.5 times increase in the number units within a period of 11 years. In the case of employment also, it increased from 2,76,127 in 1987-88 to 7,89,421 in 1997-98 which shows that the employment increased by about three times in the case of fixed investment it increased from 6,258 million in 1987-88 to 21,889 million in 1997-98, signifying a 3.5 times increase in fixed investment. Thus the SSI sector in Andhra Pradesh had shown a vibrant growth in respect of employment as well as fixed investment.

Another indicator of spread of SSI units is in terms of the number of units set up in backward areas. According to second All India SSI census conducted in 1987-88, out of 39,21,000 units in Andhra Pradesh, 21,81,000 units had been set up in backward areas, their percentage coming to 55.6 which compares well with all India average of 62.02 per cent. Among the various product groups, the food product group is a prominent group in the state of Andhra Pradesh besides the metal product industries group.

The SSI sector in general creates larger employment opportunities next only to agriculture. The generation of employment in the SSI sector is the highest in the food product industry followed by non- metallic mineral products and metal products. In Andhra Pradesh per unit employment was highest. (20) in units engaged in beverages, tobacco and tobacco products. Next came cotton textile products (17) non metallic meneral products (14.1), basic metal industries (13.6), and electrical machinery and parts (11.2). Per unit employment was also relatively high (10) in metropolitan area and lowest (05) in rural areas. The statewide employment distribution shows that Tamil Nadu made the maximum contribution to employment, while Andhra Pradesh had contributed 7.05 per cent.[3]

The Table 3.2 shows the development of medium and large scale units among the various districts in Andhra Pradesh, Medak district occupies the first place followed by Ranga Reddy and Hyderabad as per the number of units but the investment figures show that Visakapatnam, has the first rank for investment followed by Medak district. In the case of employment Khammam stands first followed by Medak. Thus there are 1433 units having an investment of Rs. 2519766.35 Lakhs and creating employment for 641162.

The percentage figures show that Medak has 22.39 per cent units in 1995 but it has slightly declined to 21.14 per cent in 1996. But there is a slight increase in its share of investment out of the total from 12.05 per cent to 12.17 per cent. In the case of Visakhapatnam also the percentage for number units as well as investment had declined in 1996 over 1995. Among the

Table 3.2
District-wise break-up of Large and Medium Scale Industries in 1995 and 1996 in Andhra Pradesh

District	1995					1996				
	Units	*Investments*	*Precentage*	*Empoy-ment*	*Percent*	*Units*	*Invest-ments*	*Percentage*	*Empoy-ment*	*Percent*
Adilabad	15(1.17)	24602.00	1.00	52997	8.56	15(1.05)	24601.45	0.97	52997	8.26
Ananthapoor	36(2.82)	38635.00	1.58	11852	1.91	39(2.72)	48669.57	1.93	13262	2.06
Chittur	80(6.26)	66912.00	2.74	17826	2.88	89(6.21)	83349.73	3.30	19110	2.98
Cuddapah	15(1.17)	32705.00	1.34	5.34	0.8	15(1.05)	32705.00	1.29	5534	0.86
East Godavari	50(3.92)	170133.00	6.98	194.67	3.14	54(3.77)	110402.60	4.38	20313	3.16
Guntur	35(2.74)	40142.00	1.64	11735	1.89	41(2.86)	44783.75	1.77	124.95	1.94
Hyderabad	119(3.92)	52256.00	2.14	25356	4.09	147(10.26)	55235.03	2.19	27367	4.26
Karimnagar	11(0.86)	123207.00	5.50	40426	6.53	12(0.84)	123432.00	4.89	40444	6.30
Khammam	22(1.72)	153968.00	6.31	149987	24.25	22(1.54)	151301.00	6.00	149987	23.39
Krishna	47(3.68)	37481.00	1.53	18439	2.98	51(3.56)	38709.45	1.53	18700	2.91
Kurnool	24(1.88)	21778.00	0.89	10148	1.64	27(1.88)	24600.00	0.97	10377	1.61
M.Bub Nagar	40(3.13)	27179.00	11.15	6551	1.05	42(2.93)	31455.46	11.24	7285	1.13
Medak	286(22.39)	293881.00	12.05	66505	10.75	303(21.14)	320461.58	12.17	68464	10.67

(Contd...)

Nalgonda	91(7.13)	107438.00	4.04	19695	3.18	106(7.4)	161673.54	6.41	24612	3.83
Nellore	45(3.52)	32255.00	1.32	10258	1.65	53(3.7)	37241.75	1.47	11621	1.81
Nizamabad	12(0.94)	7591.00	0.31	3793	0.61	13(0.91)	7895.00	0.31	3853	0.60
Prakasham	18(1.1)	12941.00	0.53	5874	0.94	21(1.46)	16331.64	0.64	6651	1.03
Ranga Reddy	180(14.09)	217047.00	8.90	63343	10.24	218(15.21)	230910.02	9.16	67276	10.49
Srikakulam	15(1.17)	12193.00	0.50	3666	0.59	20(1.4)	12922.76	0.51	4029	0.62
Visakapatnam	66(5.17)	900204.00	36.94	46309	7.48	69(4.81)	893501.67	35.45	46563	7.26
Vijayanagaram	19(1.49)	30312.00	1.24	12564	2.03	20(1.39)	31673.68	1.25	12681	1.97
Warangal	15(1.17)	1147.00	0.46	3356	0.54	17(1.18)	12075.93	0.47	3458	0.53
W.godavari	36(2.82)	22634.00	0.92	12799	2.06	39(2.72)	25833.74	1.05	14089	2.19
Total	**1277(99.97)**	**2436929.00**	**101.84**	**618480**	**99.87**	**1433**	**2519766.35**	**99.35**	**641162**	**89.55**

Source: Government of Andhra Pradesh, Commissionerate of Industries, Hyderabad.

Table 3.3(a)
Smale Scale Industries in Andhra Pradesh (Permanently Registered)
As on 31.03.1997

Category	*Units (Rs. in Crores)*	*Invest-ments*	*Percentage*	*Employ-ment*	*Percentage*
Food Processing	30394 (24.7)	558.40	26.04	239263	22.39
Beverages & Tobacco Products	1385(1.12)	25.07	1.16	56557	5.29
Textiles	2457(1.98)	41.08	1.91	27271	2.55
Wood Products	11759(9.47)	46.75	2.18	63893	5.97
Paper Products & Printing	8015(6.45)	1123.31	5.28	51571	4.82
Leather & Leather Products	3232(2.60)	18.28	0.85	15591	1.45
Rubber, Plastic And Petrolium Products	5957(4.79)	184.73	8.61	42006	3.93
Chemical & Allied Industries	5158(4.15)	232.31	10.83	77099	7.21
Mineral Base Industries	10821(8.71)	246.24	11.48	167125	15.64
Basic Metal Industries	1938(1.56)	130.66	6.09	30305	2.83
Metal Products	12656(10.19)	137.19	6.31	96725	9.05
Machinery Equipments	9476(7.63)	137.49	6.41	63647	5.95
Electrical & Electronics	3059(2.46)	79.55	3.71	31216	2.92
Transport Equipments & Parts	2085(1.68)	32.34	1.50	17311	1.62
Miscellaneous	1803(1.45)	18.69	0.87	13846	1.29
Repairing	12845(10.34)	108.61	1.06	61594	5.76
Others	1169(0.94)	3.40	1.55	13415	1.25
Total	**124209(99.99)**	**2144.10**	**99.84**	**1068482**	**99.92**

Source: Government of Andhra Pradesh, Commissionerate of Industries, Hyderabad.

Table 3.3 (b)

Particulars of Category-wise Break-up of SIDO Units Peramenently Registered as on 31-12-1999

Cat. No.	*Category*	*No. of Units*	*Investemnts (Rs in Crores)*	*Percentage*	*Employ-ment*	*Percent-age*
20,21	Food Processing	31814(23.55)	779.87	24.47	255450	21.65
22	Beverages & Tobacco Products	1446(1.07)	33.71	1.05	18866	4.98
23,24,25,26	Textiles	2594(1.92)	79.32	2.48	33403	2.83
27	Wood Products	12375(9.16)	65.89	2.06	6747	5.71
28	Paper Products & Printing	8673(6.42)	156.77	4.92	56232	4.76
29	Leather & Leather Products	3341(2.47)	24.37	0.76	16764	1.42
30	Rubber, Plastic And Petrolium Products	6555(4.85)	320.15	10.04	49388	4.18
31	Chemical & Allied Industries	6062(4.49)	397.73	1.48	88442	7.49
32	Mineral Base Industries	1034(8.91)	339.15	10.64	187044	15.85
33	Basic Metal Industries	2154(1.59)	157.50	4.94	33578	2.84
34	Metal Products	13180(9.76)	183.54	5.76	101517	8.60
35	Machinery Equipments	10353(7.66)	194.90	6.11	69643	5.90
36	Electrical & Electronics	3743(2.77)	109.63	3.44	357.87	3.03
37	Transport Equipments & Parts	2176(1.61)	43.76	1.37	18142	1.53
38	Miscellaneous	2725(2.02)	66.96	2.10	20189	1.71
39	Repairing	13707(10.15)	120.99	3.79	65646	5.56
40	Others	2170(1.60)	111.73	3.50	22305	1.89
	Total	**135102(100.01)**	**3185.97**	**99.91**	**1179863**	**99.93**

Source: Government of Andhra Pradesh, Commissionerate of Industries, Hyderabad.

different districts Hyderabad recorded an increase in the percentage for number of units from 9.32 in 1995 to 14.26 in 1996. Its investment share had also increased from 2.14 per cent to 2.19 per cent. Among other districts Nalgonda had registered an increase in the percentage share of investment from 4.04 to 6.41, whereas Ranga Reddy has shown an increase in the percentage for units from 14.09 to 15.21 but investment only increased from 8.90 to 9.16. As regards employment, Khammam which had its share as 24.25 per cent in 1995 had registered a decline to 23.39 per cent in 1996. More than 10 per cent share in employment had been recorded in the case of Medak and Ranga Reddy where it declined from 10.75 to 10.67 in Medak, while it increased from 10.24 to 10.49 in Ranga Reddy. Though Visakhapatnam has the highest share in total investment its share in employment had declined from 7.48 per cent 1995 to 7.26 per cent in 1996. Thus there had not been much change in the relative shares of different districts either in the pattern of investment or pattern of employment.

Table 3.3 shows the small scale Industries in different lines of activity as on 31.3.1997 and 31.12.1999.

Among the various units, the percentage for Food processing units is the highest in 1997 as well as 1999 but there is a slight decline from 24.14 per cent to 23.55. The share of units in other lines of activity like chemical and allied industries, Mineral based industries, basic metal industries have shown some improvement in their percentage. Likewise machinery and equipment, electrical and electronics have also shown an improvement in the percentage in 1999 over 1997. In the share of investment by different units the share had shown a declining tendency in the case of Food processing. But in the case of Textiles it had shown improvement and another line of activity where improvement is more than 1.00 per cent is rubber, plastics and petroleum products. Similarly chemical and allied industries have also registered a 1.00 per cent increase in their share. In the case of other lines of activity though there had been some increase in their share out of the total number of units, their percentage in the Total investment had been steadily

Table 3.4

Particulars of District-wise Small Scale Industries Permanently Registered as on 31-12-1999

District Code	*District*	*Units*	*Investments*	*Percentage*	*Employment*	*Percent*
	Adilabad	1667(1.23)	30.67	0.96	15079	1.27
	Ananthapoor	4386(3.25)	79.96	2.50	37658	3.19
	Chittur	3657(2.71)	93.51	2.93	33414	2.83
	Cuddapah	3640(2.69)	53.66	1.68	31548	2.67
	East Godavari	7789(5.77)	181.17	5.68	67289	5.70
	Guntur	6605(4.89)	197.18	6.18	63394	5.37
	Hyderabad	1289(9.52)	164.64	1.16	100594	8.52
	Karimnagar	4563(3.38)	105.77	3.31	41687	3.53
	Khammam	4170(3.09)	71.97	2.29	36333	3.07
	Krishna	8040(5.95)	214.4	6.72	72672	6.15
	Kurnool	4066(3.01)	79.21	2.48	34711	2.94
	M.Bub Nagar	3036(2.25)	62.36	1.95	24140	2.04
	Medak	4071(2.01)	191.16	6.00	40304	2.41

Nalgonda	7018(5.19)	162.97	5.11	65575	5.55
Nellore	947(4.40)	79.71	2.50	58083	4.92
Nizamabad	3698(2.74)	55.02	1.72	33417	2.83
Prakasham	4710(3.49)	82.48	2.58	41916	3.5
Ranga Reddy	14931(11.05)	681.40	21.38	132009	11.18
Srikakulam	4568(3.38)	84.82	2.66	38977	3.30
Visakapatnam	9851(7.29)	219.82	6.89	76087	6.44
Vijayanagaram	3281(2.43)	56.59	1.77	28552	2.41
Warangal	5984(4.43)	75.90	2.38	47602	4.03
W. Godavari	6565(4.85)	161.60	1.07	56822	4.81
Total	**135102(100.00)**	**3185.97**	**99.86**	**1179863**	**99.71**

Source: Government of Andhra Pradesh, Commissionerate of Industries, Hyderabad.

declining. In the case of employment also there is a decline in the percentage for Food processing units, but there is an increase in the share for Textiles and Rubber products.

Even in the case of chemical industries and Mineral based industries, and Electrical goods industries there is a slight increase in the share for employment. Among different lines of activity, after Food processing which still had 21.65 percent out of total employment, Mineral based industries have a higher share when compared with other lines of activity as its share is 50.85 per cent in 1999. Thus Rubber products, chemical and Mineral based industries are slowly improving their relative shares in employment.

Table 3.4 shows the district-wise data of small scale Industries permanently registered as on 31-12-1999. Among the units located in different districts, the highest percentage of units - 11.05 are existing in Ranga Reddy followed by Hyderabad with 9.52 per cent and Visakhapatnam with 7.29 per cent. Among other districts only Krishna, Nalgonda, and East Godavari have more than 5 per cent. When the relative shares of the investments are taken into accounts Ranga Reddy alone had 21.38 per cent of the total investments by these units in the state of A.P. Among other districts Visakhapatnam comes next with 6.89 percent followed by 6.72 percent for Krishna, 6.18 per cent for Guntur and 6.00 per cent for Medak.

Three others districts which have more than 5 per cent of total investment are East Godavari, Hyderabad, Nalgonda and West Godavari. In case of employment though Ranga Reddy has the highest percentage, it is not more than 11.18 per cent. Next comes Hyderabad with 8.52 per cent followed by 6.44 per cent for Visakhapatnam and 6.15 per cent for Krishna. Thus there is some association between the percentage for investment and percentage for employment in most of the districts, the exceptions being Ranga Reddy, Medak, Hyderabad and Nellore.

Table 3.5 shows achievements of DICs in promoting SSI and Tiny unit is from 1995-96 to 1999-2000. The performance of different districts shows that there are certain districts where

Table 3.5
Achievement of District Industries Centres in SSI /Tiny Units Set up from 1995-96 to 1999-2000

Sl.No.	District	1995-96		1996-97		1997-98		1998-99		1999-2000	
		Target	*Acheivement*	*Target*	*Acheivement*	*Target*	*Acheivement*	*Target*	*Acheivement*	*Target*	*Acheivement*
01	Adilabad	285	273	300	269	330	447	350	291	375	385
02	Ananthapoor	655	662	725	728	795	1076	835	1179	893	1326
03	Chittur	990	992	1090	1092	1200	1457	1260	1819	1348	963
04	Cuddapah	655	656	720	742	790	834	830	910	888	889
05	East Godavari	1225	967	1065	978	1170	1412	1230	1606	1316	1778
06	Guntur	1110	1147	1260	1511	1385	3641	1596	2548	1605	2371
07	Hyderabad	490	495	545	546	612	571	612	658	688	633
08	Karimnagar	650	652	715	718	785	798	785	793	840	973
09	Khammam	885	1088	1200	1372	1320	1850	1385	1126	1482	1667
10	Krishna	1505	1513	1665	1670	1830	1845	190	2000	2054	2284
11	Kurnool	790	802	885	1010	970	1267	1020	1363	1090	1507
12	M.Bub Nagar	680	726	800	808	8080	936	900	968	963	1038

(Contd...)

13	Medak	810	814	900	921	991	1316	1040	1296	1112	1401
14	Nalgonda	710	744	820	1109	900	1266	945	1266	1011	1365
15	Nellore	1080	1131	1245	1275	1370	1518	1440	1347	1541	1845
16	Nizamabad	640	670	740	756	810	922	850	913	910	966
17	Prakasham	990	1095	1200	1219	1320	1546	1320	1582	1482	1536
18	Ranga Reddy	1260	1094	1200	1386	1320	1354	1400	1595	1498	5119
19	Srikakulam	700	837	920	952	1010	1364	1060	1185	1134	1355
20	Visakhapatnam	1386	1200	1320	1667	1450	1723	1520	2136	1626	1979
21	Vijayanagaram	630	642	701	718	717	810	810	929	867	897
22	Warangal	750	481	530	522	580	656	610	818	653	752
23	W. Godavari	1085	1188	1310	1338	1440	1654	1510	1573	1616	1534
	Total	**19961**	**19869**	**21856**	**23307**	**24027**	**30263**	**25228**	**29901**	**26992**	**30963**

their achievements uniformly exceeded the targets in all the years. These districts are Anantapur, Cuddapah, Guntur, Karimnagar, Krishna, Kurnool, Mahabubnagar, Medak, Nalgonda, Nizamabad, Prakasham, Srikakulam and Vijayanagaram. In the case of other districts where they could not reach the target, their achievements were more than compensating in other years. East Godavari could not achieve its targets in the first two years. But in the later year its achievement was much better. Among all the districts the achievements were spectacular in the case of Guntur where it consistently over reached its target sequentially in three years that is 1997-98, 1998-99 and 1999-2000.

Year	*Target*	*Achievement*
1995-96	19961	19869
1996-97	21856	23307
1997-98	24027	30263
1998-99	25228	29901
1999-2000	26992	30963
Total	**118064**	**134303**

Source: Government of Andhra Pradesh, Commissionerate of Industries, Hyderabad.

Thus the DICs have registered a better performance in certain districts like Guntur, Khammam, Kurnool, Medak, Nellore, Visakhapatnam, and to a certain extent in Srikakulam and Ananthapur.

Thus there is a vigorous drive to promote the SSI units and in some of the districts where there had been over-reaching of target, entrepreneurs have come forward for setting of the units under the liberalization scenario that exists in the state of Andhra Pradesh.

Traits of Entrepreneurs in Andhra Pradesh

Among the various attempts that had been made to

analyze the pattern of entrepreneurship in Andhra Pradesh, a study on emerging investors in East Godavari district of Andhra Pradesh was brought out by the Directorate of Industries, Andhra Pradesh in collaboration with the Administrative Staff College of India. The objective of survey were:

(1) To examine profile of Individuals who are potential investors in manufacturing;

2) To find the motive, attitudes and influences of individuals;

3) To examine the Industrial potential of the districts;

4) To suggest the steps to the government to take to attract capital from non-industrial sectors in the district in to small scale industries.

The size of the sample is 200, of with 35 were industrial entrepreneurs. These entrepreneurs belong to Kakinada, Rajamundry areas of East Godavari district. An analysis of data collected from with sample entrepreneurs through a questionnaire revealed the following attributes of the entrepreneurs:

1) Out of the 35 industrial entrepreneurs, 9 had come from agricultural sector and 8 from professional groups and 14 entrepreneurs belong to industry and as such they were not new entrants to industry;

2) A majority of entrepreneurs are in the age group of 35-50 years and none of them had any professional education;

3) Profit and confidence in the line were the main motives that led individuals to enter industry;

4) A majority of individuals are influenced in their decision to enter industry by their parents and family relations;

5) 29 out of 35 entrepreneurs interviewed reported that their competence and opportunities in manufacturing were principal reasons for entering Industry;

6) The entrepreneurs were influenced by visits to industrial units. Only one individual out of 35 reported that government publicity media was helpful in deciding for him to enter the field of manufacturing;

7) The initial capital requirements of the units of the sample were rupees 50,000. Most of the entrepreneurs met the requirements from their own personal resources and only one obtained financial assistance from the govt.;

8) The management of the unit was by the family members of the entrepreneur with technical background in some cases;

9) 16 out of 35 entrepreneurs reported that they were planning to expand the operations by diversifying into new product;

10) Only 10 out of 35 individuals reported incidents of labour unrest in their units;

11) Other issues were facility of long term loans, raw Material shortage, lack of market for finished products. As for the break even period of new enterprises, the survey shows that the period ranges between one to three years. Some entrepreneurs reported that the government controls were standing in the way for the firm to operate under normal conditions. A majority of entrepreneurs reported material shortage as the major problem, which was responsible for impeding a better performance.

12) The replies of the entrepreneurs to questions regarding various institutions assistance meant for helping the small industry revealed a complete confusion in their minds on the available sources of help in respect of labour, technical know-how and raw material supplies. In respect of finances however the entrepreneurs were clear about the sources they should approach.

The report had given the following recommendations:

1. Department of Industries should do product research to identify profitable manufacturing lines;
2. Opportunities and profit in manufacturing should be the central theme of the department in its communications;
3. A complete holiday should be given from all the accountabilities to new entrepreneurs;
4. Department should extend the range of services presently offered. It should cease to be simple licensing body;
5. Confusion in the minds of individuals on the sources of guidance should be removed;
6. Guided visits should be arranged externsively to help the entrepreneurs;
7. Demonstration effect is very powerful and it should be exploited;
8. Social image of entrepreneurs should be improved;
9. Publicity strategy of the department should be redrawn;
10. Information relations with various categories of population, particularly with moneylenders are useful and should be used;

Small Industry Extension Training Institute, Hyderabad had undertaken a study of entrepreneurs in the small scale industrial sector in twin cities of Hyderabad and Secunderabad.[5] The study is based on the analysis of information collected from entrepreneurs. The purpose of the study was to determine the influence of selected biographical, sociological and psychological factors on the adoption of the innovation of starting a small scale Industrial unit. Major conclusions of the study are as given hereunder:

1) 75 per cent of the respondents were between 31 and

50 years of age, whereas 44 per cent were between 31 and 40 years and 31 per cent were between 41 and 50 years. The typical entrepreneur was of 39 years age.

2) 80 per cent of the respondents were Hindus, 18 per cent were Muslims and 2 per cent Christians.

3) 41 per cent of the respondents had college degrees and 33 per cent had passed high school; 26 per cent of the respondents had technical education. Thus the typical entrepreneur had formal college education.

4) The typical entrepreneur belonged to a family with middle or low income group. Thus among entrepreneur 28 per cent , 25 per cent and 23 per cent belonged to families with monthly income in ranges of Rs. 500 to Rs. 999, Rs. 200 to Rs. 499, Rs. 1,000 to Rs. 1,499 respectively.

5) 66 per cent of the respondents were local resident and 34 per cent came from outside Secunderabad and Hyderabad and 89 per cent of respondents came from cities.

6) 61 per cent of the respondents had experience in industry, while another 8 per cent were engaged in business dealing with items similar to what they manufactured later.

The reasons for starting industrial units had been mentioned by the entrepreneurs:

1) For all the 61 respondents, economic gains were the most important reason for starting the small industry unit. Second most important reason was own ambition. The third and fourth most important reasons were social prestige and social responsibility.

2) Respondents with high adoption propensity differed considerably in their reasons for starting the industrial units. For Respondents with high adoption propensity, own ambition was the most important reason for starting the industrial units followed by

economic gain, inventions and social prestige, while for the other groups economic gains were the most important reason for starting the industrial units.

3) Risk taking ability did not influence the respondent in their reason for starting the industrial units. Hence there was no relationship between reason for starting the industrial unit and time taken to adopt the innovation.

The emerging factor for starting industrial unit was the high demand for the product perceived by the entrepreneur. Another encouraging factor was experience in the line and the assistance and encouragement received from friends and family.

On the other hand capital shortage and government redtapism were seen as the most discouraging factors in starting their industrial units. The other discouraging factors are non-availability of raw materials and manpower.

The entrepreneurs also mentioned about the visits to the general organisations and assistance they received for starting small industry units. In this regard the responses were:

1) 79 per cent of the respondents mentioned visiting the office of the Directorate of Industries,
2) 56 per cent of the respondents visited the small industries services institute.
3) 20 per cent of the respondents visited the District Industries Office and 18 per cent of the respondents visited the Regional Research Laboratory,
4) The most frequently visited organisation for the 61 respondents was the Small Industries Service Institute followed by the Directorate of Industries,
5) The largest amount of assistance was received from the Directorate of Industries followed by the Small Industries Service Institute,
6) The Directorate of Industries was approached in the case of majority of the respondents for assistance in

licences, location of sites, raw materials, registration etc., and

7) The Small Industries Service Institute was approached by the majority of the respondents for technical assistance, assistance in the purchase of raw materials and machinery and for obtaining technical literature.

Role of Financial Institutions for Entrepreneurship Development

In Andhra Pradesh many financial institutions especially those which are assisting SSI Sector are functioning since the formation of Andhra Pradesh. The first step was the establishment of Andhra Pradesh State Finance Corporation in 1956 to provide long term funds to the small and medium scale industries. Later in 1960 Andhra Pradesh Industrial Development Corporation (APIDC) was set up not only to supplement financing function of APSFC but also undertake promotional activities. It conducted industrial surveys, obtained letters of intents and started manufacturing enterprises as its subsidiaries. Later in 1970 it assumed a new role of lending term loans to medium and large scale units under IDBI's refinance scheme. It also became the agent of IDBI to channelise risk capital to the technocrat/ first generation entrepreneurs under the seed capital scheme besides it also took up the responsibility of distributing central and state subsidies.

In 1961, a separate agency, the Andhra Pradesh States Small Industries Development Corporation (APIDC) was set up to exclusively address to the needs of small Scale units. It mainly assists small units in the procurement of machinery on hire purchase basis, procurement of scarce raw material and marketing of their products. Of late it has started providing risk capital to private entrepreneur. However, this is done in few deserving cases to encourage new technology, new product and a first generation entrepreneur. In 1973 the State Govt (A.P.) created the industrial infrastructure corporation (APIIC) to help the industrialists acquire well equipped sites for industrial establishments. The Corporation is engaged in developing industrial estates and construction of factory sheds with all infrastructure and offer them to entrepreneurs at the reasonable rate.

Besides the institutional arrangements at the state level, financial support is made available to industry directly by the central financial institutions such as IDBI, ICICI, DTI, and Insurance companies, usually under a consortium. There are other institutions like SBI and other nationalised banks rendering financial assistance to the entrepreneurs.

Andhra Pradesh Industrial Development Corporation (APIDC) has emerged as an important organ of the State Government to foster industrial growth in the state. The corporation adopted several functions of another organisation that is Industrial Trust Fund. Like Industrial Trust Fund the APIDC in its earlier phases followed the same procedure to lure the private capital into industry. This arrangement, later came to be known as the joint sector approach. Thus the concept of joint sector was in vogue in the state much before a national policy on it was announced by Government of India in 1973. The first joint sector enterprise in the state, the Associated Glass Industries Limited with APIDC support was incorporated in 1964. The Gangappa Cables Limited in which APIDC participated to the extent of 50 percent of the share capital came into being in 1965. This was followed by ALKALI Metal Limited in 1968, in which APIDC shared 50 per cent of the equity capital. The number of such enterprises gradually increased to 96 as at the end of March, 1987.[6]

A joint sector enterprise comes in to existence in different forms, the APIDC assumes the role of a promoter, identifies project, obtain industrial licenses and executes the project with or without a private entrepreneur. In doing so it is broadly guided by the industrial policy of the central government and commitment of state government to different regions with in the state. A JSE is straight away conceived and promoted if the IDC can identify a suitable copromotor. As an alternative, the corporation implements a project as a fully owned subsidiary and as and when a suitable private entrepreneur is identified, the day to day management is transferred in his favour. In the Third case the project is conceived by a private entrepreneur, the industrial licence is held by him and he approaches APIDC for joint participation in the risk capital. Such a proposal may come from a new venture or an established one. A joint sector enterprise may also come into being at the instance of central financial institutions. Getting licences for industrial goods was a difficult task in the 1970s, but state level agency like Industrial Development Corporations were the prefered agencies for licence allotment which in turn distributed them among the private entrepreneurs. In issuing licences the licencing authority made it conditional to use some of them to promote the venture in joint sector. As a result, some of the IDCS in the country systematically used the instrument of joint sector to secure as many licences as possible for the state concerned. The APIDC obtained as many as 113 licences/DGTD registration until May, 1987, of which 62 (50%) were used while others lapsed of the 62 used for project implementation 24 (39 percent) were in joint sector.

An evaluation of joint sector enterprises shows that not many were successful. One reason had been the caste and the political affiliations of entrepreneurs seemed to have an important bearing on the selection of entrepreneurs and the subsequent treatment of the project. Further the failures were essentially because of machinery / Technology or shortcomings of the entrepreneurs. The paper industry is a case in point where the imported machinery uniformly failed to operate at the rated capacity. The assumption made with regard to raw material also proved wrong in its case. Technology failure or machinery breakdown was a common problem with chemical plants trying with new technology. A large proportion of Joint sector enterprises were also unsuccessful because of indifferent interest shown by the entrepreneurs. In a few cases their dubious intentions were established. In some cases premature withdrawal of concessions assured by the state government led to the closure of the units. Further some of the projects linked with public sector undertakings could not do well following avoidable disputes.[7]

As the institutions have played a major role in creating these production entities, they have shown concern for their continuation and retrieval of public money involved in them. The curative action varied across the enterprise but with one commonality. In almost all the cases where the original entrepreneurs proved to be ineffective, a change of management in favour of relatively better experienced and financially strong entrepreneurs was contemplated with a package of concessions and reliefs unlike in the first selection, consideration of nativity was a relegated to the background at the time takeovers. In a few cases they were handed over to big industrial groups in contravention with the object of joint sector policy.[8]

Apart from the failure, there are some notable successes. It may be stated that the additional capacities created and the investment generated by these successful companies perhaps more than compensate the loss sustained in the sick companies having potential to create spin off effects on industrial expansion in the state. Mention may be made of Nagarjuna, Raasi and (SOL) Standard Organic Ltd. groups. Nagarjuna is a diversified group having interest in engineering, cement, fertilizers, finance and investments. Raasi though intially concentrated on cement and cement products and has since diversified into paper, finance and leasing. SOL groups is highly concentrated in drugs and pharmaceuticals. Certain issues that have come of in the development of joint sector are relevant for the growth of entrepreneurship in Andhra Pradesh. Firstly it needs to be closely examined whether the implicit policy of state government/APIDC to encourage only local entrepreneurs is tenable. Secondly a proof have to be made whether providing implicit and explicit subsides is the only way of attracting new class of entrepreneurs or there could be alternative use by which encouragement may be given to entrepreneurs.[9] Thus a review of the policy is needed in promoting entrepreneurship in the state.

In view of the policy changes required different agencies

in the state have been simplifying their procedures for encouraging entrepreneur to set up new unit. In 1998 the Andhra Pradesh government had introduced a bill named as Andhra Pradesh Small Scale Industry (Development and Simplification of Procedures) Bill 1998.[10] Under this bill there will be an establishment at state level and district level small scale industries development authority. At the state level the Commissioner of Industries, Andhra Pradesh shall be the Chairman of the authority, to bring more coordination and also to oversee the time bound clearance by the concerned officers in the matter of according approvals, granting permission and issuing license or certificate to the units of small scale industries in the state. This authority consists of not less than 9 and not more than 12 members. In this particular authority some are to be nominated by the government from among the chief executives of the Andhra Pradesh Small Scale Industrial Development Corporation, Andhra Pradesh Industrial Development Corporation, Andhra Pradesh Industrial Infrastructure Corporation and Andhra Pradesh Pollution Control Board.

According to the new provisions a provisional certificate of registration will be issued to every entrepreneur who is willing to establish a small scale industrial unit in a District within 30 days from the date of receipt of the application by the authority. A provisional certificate or registration issued by the government shall be valid for a period of 5 years and shall be renewable for after a period of 2 years at a time. Every entrepreneur, who holds a provisional certificate or registration in respect of a small scale industrial unit may, within 6 months after the unit is commissioned can make an application to the concerned industries development authority for the issue of a permanent certificate of registration in respect of said units, and they shall, after ensuring that production facilities have actually been established, issue a permanent certificate of registration to the entrepreneur of the unit forthwith. For this purpose the District Small Scale Industries Development Authority, with the general manager of the DIC as the Chairman of the authority will be responsible.

Once the permanent certificate of registration has been issued, each industrial unit shall be entitled to claim on priority basis all the facilities and benefits that may from time to time be allowed to small scale or Tiny Industry.[11]

Besides the simplification of the procedure, the financial institutions also step into forward help to the SSI centre. In 1999 SIDBI has reduced the minimum quantum of financial assistance from Rs. 20 lakh to Rs. 10 Lakh for marketing of SSI products and delegate the powers of sanction for non-traditional lines of activities shall be applicable for assistance under the marketing scheme. The APSFC has framed the objective to provide financial assistance to a SSI unit to undertake various activities to increase their turnover in domestic and exports markets. The second objective is to finance service providers which provide support services and/or infrastructure facilities to small scale sector to improve its marketing capability. For this particular purpose existing SSI units in the small scale sector with a good track record and good sound financial position are eligible for financial assistance. However new units will also be considered on a selective basis. The minimum quantum of financial assistance shall be Rs. 20 lakh for borrowals including working capital term loan. However the cost of the project should not exceed Rs. 500 Lakh and it may include land, building, showroom facilities, office equipments, core working capital, and regional expenses to be incurred on publicity. The debt-equity ratio shall not exceed 2:1. The loan eligibility is 65 per cent of the cost of eligible components of the project including core working capital. A minimum of 17 per cent premium plus interest tax will be collected from time to time. A special interest rebate at the rate of 2 per cent per annum shall be allowed for the loans sanctioned towards assistance for marketing of SSI products at the time of closure of loan Account. The term loan shall be repaid in quarterly instalment with in a maximum period of Five years with moratorium of one year.[12]

Andhra Pradesh State Financial Corporation is the prime term lending institution extending financial assistance to set up industrial venture in tiny, small scale and medium scale sector in Andhra Pradesh state.[13] The main objectives of the corporation in respect of the small scale industry (SSI) sector are to accelerate the industrial growth of the state in SSI sector, increased employment generation; optimum utilisation of potential resources available in the state for industrial development in SII Sector; improve export potential and diagnose industrial sickness in SSI sector and assist the sick industries to recover from sickness. In order to achieve the objective the strategy proposed by the corporation is as follows:

1) To promote infrastructure for development of SSI Sector,
2) To identify potential lines of activities and effective promotion of industries in these lines,
3) To create proper organisational arrangements.
4) To utilise funds available under various schemes like NEF, MUN, SC/ST component plan etc., for development of industries,
5) Simplification of procedures for quick sanction and timely sustenance to entrepreneurs, and
6) Conducting development campaigns and participating in entrepreneurial development programmes.

APSFC the strategy includes identification of thrust areas for promoting investment in small scale sector in the state the following thrust areas have been identified keeping in view the availability of raw materials, market potential and other factors of production:

1) Agro based and food processing industries,
2) Pharmaceutical formulations,
3) Chemical and chemical based industries,
4) Electronics, computer software and hardware,
5) Mineral based industries.

6) Engineering industry.
7) Plastics processing, and
8) Linear and non-linear computer animation.

The Andhra Pradesh industrial sector, according to Vision 2020, is expected to grow at 11 per cent a year in real terms.[14] For this Andhra Pradesh will need a total investment of roughly Rs. 11,65,000 crores. Most of this investment will have to be raised through private investment. The growth thrust will focus on 3 types of industries: Knowledge based, resource-based, and labour intensive. Knowledge based industries include Information Technology, bio-technology and pharmaceuticals. Resource based industries include mining, construction and agro industry. Labour intensive industries include garments and leather products. These are considered growth engines which are expected to foster development of small scale industries. For instance construction and pharmaceuticals are expected to give rise to many opportunities for the small industry.

It is expected that by 2020 Andhra Pradesh will have many dynamic and profitable small scale industries.

Propelled by technological development and capability building, small scale industries will receive an impetus in the state. The proliferation of these industries will provide many opportunities of entrepreneurship and employment. The approach[15] to developing small scale industries will focus on:

- Building skills and promoting technological development,
- Providing infrastructure and credit,
- Reforming policy and simplifying procedure,
- Providing assistance with marketing and,
- Encouraging the development of special categories of entrepreneurs, women, scheduled castes, and tribes, backward classes.

Figure 4
Schemes for Financial Assistance

Scheme	*Eligibility*	*Purpose*	*Remarks*
1. Assistance to A" & A' Good Entrepreneur	Existing assisted units of corporation Good entrepreneur under A++ category of existing units assisted by corporation, in operation for more than three years, earned net profits during last three years and regular in repayments to the Corporation without availing reschedulement facility during last three years. Good entrepreneurs under A+ category of existing units assisted by the corporation satisfying the criteria under A++ category and who have not availed reschedulement facility more than once.	For acquiring additional assets for expansion, technology up gradation & diversification, and/or for working capital term loan.	Networth: Not exceeding Rs. 12.00 crores. A^{++}Category: Interest concesion 1% and Lower Promoters margins. A^{+}Category: Interest concesion 1/2% and Lower Promoters margins. A-1Category:Interest concesion 0.50% and Lower Promoters margins. A-2Category:Interest concesion 0.25% and Lower Promoters margins.

(Contd...)

A - 1	Existing units which have closed loan account with the corporation, or existing units not assisted by the corporation but satisfying by the norms of A++ or A+		Working Capital Term Loan: For sale proprietory & Paertnership forms: Rs. 120 Lakhs. For Pvt & Public Ltd.
A-2	New units promoted by promoters with 51% or more stake in existing A++ or A+ and seeking assistance with 51% financial stake.	(New units under A-2 category are not eligible for working captial term loan.)	Companies: Rs. 240 Lakhs.
2. Super Entrepreneur Scheme.	For outstanding entrepreneurs in existence for atleast 10 years with the corporation for minimum aggregate of 5 years, earning net profits for the past 3 years and cash profits atleast for 2 years without any cash loses. For working capital term loans. The turnover shall be to an extenet of 400 % of the laon on an average for 3 years with the networth at least 150% of the loan amount.	For acquiring fixed assets required for expansion, diversification etc. For working captial requirements. For only other business industrial need other than for speculative purposes.	Terms Loans: Sale Proprietory/ Partnership Firm : upto Rs. 120 Lakhs. Private & Public Limited companies up to Rs. 240 lakh. In case of both, the overall sanctions limits shall not exceed the prescribed limits of term loans.

(Contd...)

3. Senior Successful Entrepreneur Scheme.	For outstanding entrepreneurs in existence for a minimum period of 10 years and not availed financial assistance from corporation, earning net profits for atleast 5 years with cash profits, having no accumulated cash losses.	-For acquiring fixed asets requried for expansion, modernisation, diversification etc. -For working capital requirements.	Term Loans: Sole propritory/partnership Firm: up to Rs. 120 lakh Private & public Ltd. Companies up to : Rs. 240 lakh working captial term loans: Sale proprietory / partnership firms: upto : Rs. 120 lakh. private & public ltd. companies: upto Rs. 240 lakh. In case of both, the overall sanction limits shall not exceed the prescribed limtis of term loans.
4. Equipment Refinance Scheme.	Existing will performing small and medium scale units: - Assited by the corporation, or by any other state/ central financial institution. Bank/self - financed. - Units should be in operation for at least 4 years from the date of	For acquiring identifiable items of plant and machinery/other equipments including energy saving systems, for modernization. expansion balancing/ replacement or any other purpose except new project.	Project cost including proposed equipment, showed not exceed Rs. 12.00 crores.

(Contd...)

	commercial production, earned profits/ declared dividends, during immediate preceding 2 years, not defoulte in repayment to institutions / bank.		
5. Moderniza-tion Scheme	Existing tiny, village, small and medium scale units which are in operation atleast for 5 years. In caste of replacement / renovation the machinery showed have been in use in the unit for a period atleast 5 years.	Assistance for modernization. - DP gradation of process/ Product technology & product. - Export oriented - Import-substitution. - Energy saving.	Total project cost: Not to exceed Rs. 12 crores.

In keeping with the general policy towards the development of small scale sector, and its policy to develop women and disadvantaged groups, entrepreneurship among these groups will be encouraged in the following ways.

First emphasis will be laid on identifying industrial activity suitable to areas in which disadvantaged groups live, and to the creation of infrastructure augmentation of credit and capability building for these groups. This will include helping them to acquire technical and managerial skills through training programmes to ensure access to credit, and the state government will encourage the setting up of local area banks and exclusive banks for women. Second, entrepreneurs from disadvantaged groups will be offered special fiscal concessions such as enhanced tax limits.[16]

In consonance with the dynamic scenario, different state level organisations are coming forward with new schemes to encourage entrepreneurship in the state. APSFC will be now giving more general loans for all proprietary, partnership, private/public Limited companies and to industrial co-operative societies for establishing tiny, small scale industrial units and service oriented industries. The purpose for which loan would be given is for acquiring assets, for setting up new units and for expansion, diversification and modernisation in case of existing units. The project cost should not exceed Rs. 12 crores. Further the Corporation has a gradation of entrepreneurs for the provision of Financial Assistance. The table (Fig. 4) shows how the corporation will be assisting entrepreneurs.[17]

For 2000-2001, the APSFC has modified its lending policy under three categories namely open, Restricted and not to be encouraged categories. Loans below Rs. 5 lakhs shall be given low priority except in the cases of transport loans, tourism related activity and other special schemes likes Mahila Udhyama Nidhi, National Equity Fund, SEMFEX and Women entrepreneur schemes. If a particular line of activity is not listed in any of the above three categories of lending policy prior approval may be obtained and financial assistance will be considered by the Corporation where there are no sick units.

For all lines of activity listed under open category, a minimum collateral security of 25 per cent of the term loan shall be insisted, for giving encouragement to the entrepreneur. In the case of all lines of activities listed under restricted categories a minimum collateral security of 50 per cent will be insisted. In respect of units being set up in industrial estates, collateral security shall be insisted on the extent of loans or machinery only, since it is easy to sell the land and building in case of default. For additional term loan being considered to existing good entrepreneur, no collateral security is to be insisted, unless the risk perception so warrants.[18]

For additional term loans to existing entrepreneurs, coming up for expansion/diversification or modernization collateral security of 25 per cent on additional term loan is to be insisted for those lines of activities listed under open and restricted category for which higher collateral security is insisted for new entrepreneurs, unless risk perception warrants higher collateral security. In the case of loans being considered to Nursing Homes/Hospitals the collateral security shall be at the rate of 100 per cent on electro-medical equipment, furniture etc. only and collateral security is not be insisted on land and Buildings.[19]

Likewise the minimum promoters' contribution for all lines of activity listed under open and restricted category shall be a 25 per cent of eligible assets proposed in the project, however subject to DER norms for individual projects. Financial Assistance shall be considered with a maximum DER of 3:1 for project consisting less than Rs. 10 Lakh and a maximum of 2:1 for project costing above Rs. 10 Lakh as per SIDBI/IDBI finance guidelines.[20]

Thus the APSFC will be exceeding financial assistance to entrepreneurs in different lines of activity for promotion of entrepreneurship in the state.

Another state level organisation, Andhra Pradesh Industrial Infrastructure Corporation (APIIC) had also been expanding its activities to assist the entrepreneurs. Over the years it has built a network of industrial areas in the state; the latest being industries specific parks like growth centres, export promotion industrial park and apparel export park. APIIC is also the agency for taking up internationally funded project be it ADB sponsored or World Bank added as per international standards. Recently APIIC has set a precedent by floating a joint venture company with the L & T for the development of hightech city in Madhapur near Hyderabad to provide infrastructure for information technology in Andhra Pradesh. Likewise they have also planned to develop an industrial park at Parvada in Visakhapatnam to encourage entrepreneurship in the growing metropolitan area in Visakhapatnam. The fiscal incentives now provided are as follows:

I) State subsidy @ 20 per cent on Fixed capital Investment subject to a ceiling of Rs. 20.00 Lakh,

II) Sales Tax exemption deferment for 7/14 years up to 135 per cent of fixed capital investment;.

III) 25 per cent power rebate on power bills for a period of 3 years subject to a limit of Rs. 30.00 lakh for SSI,

IV) Investment subsidy of 20 per cent upto Rs. 20.00 lakh for captive power plants up to 1500 KVA capacity,

V) Sales Tax reduced to 4 per cent on diesel used for captive power generation.

VI) For mega projects with investment above Rs. 200 crores on case to case basis.[21]

Further the APIIC has also embarked on construction of Mega Industrial Infrastructure Park like Parvada at other prime location in the state. Its latest venture in association with the central government is export promotion industrial park (EPIP) at Pashamyllaram, 30 km away from capital city of Hyderabad. This high potential industrial park holds out more prospects to exporters with a minimum export requirement of 33 per cent of their overall turnover.

Among other institutions that had been striving to develop entrepreneurship in Andhra Pradesh is Andhra Pradesh

Industrial and Technical Consultancy Organisatoin Ltd. (APITCO). APITCO is a single window public sector undertaking, a joint venture of financial institutions like the IDBI, ICICI, IFC, APIDP, PSFC, APSFC, APSSIDC and nationalized Banks like State Bank of India, Syndicate Bank, Indian Bank and Andhra Bank. Its aim is to bridge the gap between the entrepreneur and the financial institutions. APITCO escorted more than 9000 entrepreneurs so far through various commercially viable projects. 85 per cent of these units have been operative profitably and have gone in for expansion and diversifications progammes on their own right. From concept to commissioning this involves market survey, organising of technology transfer, arrangement of Fiancees and buy back, preparation of tecfhno commercial feasibility report, project appraisal through financial institutions, procurements and installation of plant and machinery. startup, Trial runs, Quality Assurance and finally commercial production. APITCO has been offering technical assistance in the following sectors[22].

1) Computer software/End Use computing projects like E-Commerce, Medical Transcription etc.,
2) Infrastructure sector like power, Telecommunications and Highways,
3) Post Harvest Management of crops and cold storage,
4) Fruits and Vegetable processing,
5) Cereal Foods and snacks,
6) Dairy industry,
7) Bio-technology,
8) Non-conventional sources of energy,
9) Receiving and sending international delegates for technology transfers, equity participation and buy back,
10) Even Management like organising and conducting national/international seminars and other programmes like,

a) Entrepreneur Development,

b) Management Development,

c) Skill Development,

d) Attitudinal Development,

11) Power generation and manufacture of Bio-fertilizers from municipal waste,

12) Energy Audit programmes and conservation studies for industrial units,

13) Conduct of Energy Conservation Awareness programmes,

14) Waste Minimisation studies and implementation of cost effective measures.

APITCO had also been a catelyst in technology transfer in the area of plastics, edible oil refining, castor seed processing, Bulk drugs and chemicals. It had been very active in implementing a detailed plan for modenization of the cluster units in the areas of fruit processing, packaging, Marketing and developing the skill of workers. This organisation is also active in the flotation of appropriate and innovating rural technology. Further it has effected transfer of low cost appropriate technology to benefit small and tiny sector in the leather, Hosiery and silk units in the state. It has also been assigned the task of popuralising right specific Rural Technologies in select districts of the state by the government of Andhra Pradesh.

APITCO has organised over 20 energy conservation awareness programme for the benefit of local industrialists and engineers at the district level throughout Andhra Pradesh. It has also conducted in-plant Training programmes on energy conservation and management for plant operators, engineers and management in large industrial undertakings. This organisatioin has also formulated comprehensive turn around packages for 90 sick industrial units covering a diverse range of products like plastics, edible oil refining and general engineering. It is also a driving force behind the development of export strategies for industrial units tapping the overseas market.[23]

The above emerging perspective on the industrial scene of Andhra Pradesh unravels the integrated strategy for entrepreneurship development in the state. In a country like India mostly we find entrepreneurs either in the imitative category or drone category. The opening up of the economy and the globalisation trends indicate that India has to traverse a path of industrial development where entrepreneurs of risk taking nature should be developed to face the new challenges. Entrepreneurship acquired a different meaning as betting on the strong is the catchword for the various types of assistance rendered to the entrepreneurs. Hence a tough category of entrepreneurs can alone survive and prosper and the need of the hour is to intervene effectively in the entrepreneurial process for protecting the weaker among the list. In the case of entrepreneurs struggling to find a niche for themselves in the small scale sector (SSI), entrepreneurship has to be nurtured by the State.

NOTES

1. Government of Andhra Pradesh, *Vision 2020*, Swarnandra Pradesh, NISIET, Hyderabad, Chapter -xvi, pp. 271-272.
2. SIDBI, *Report on SSI Sector, 1997-98*, p. 30.
3. *Small Scale Industries in India*, January 1999.
5. *Ibid.*, pp. 81-84.
6. G. Pakki Reddy, Industrial promotion through a joint sector a study in Andhra Pradesh, Ph.D. dissertation, Osmania University, 1990, pp. 37-41.
7. *Ibid.*, pp. 248-249.
8. *Ibid.*, p. 249.
9. *Ibid.*, p. 250.
10. Industries and Commerce Dept, Govt. of A.P.
11. The benefits given to small scale units as per the this bill are shown in appendix -I of this chapter, pp. 81-85.

12. APSF, Hyderabad : Office order No. 142, dated 15 .09 1998
13. APSFC policy is shown in Appendix -II of this chapter.
14. Government of Andhra Pradesh, *Vision 2020*, Chapter-xvi, pp. 231-233.
15. The approach is explained in detailed in appendix - III.
16. Government of Andhra Pradesh, *Vision 2020*, pp. 267-272.
17. ASPFC Scheme for Financial Assistance, 1999, pp. 4-5.
18. APSFC Lending Policy 2000-2001, pp. 1-2.
19. *Ibid.*, pp. 3-4.
20. *Ibid.*, pp. 4-5.
21. APIIC a brochure on Industrial Park Parwada.
22. APITCO 9 brochure on one with the entrepreneur.
23. *Ibid.*

4

Socio-economic Profile of Entrepreneurs

Entrepreneurship Development is a forerunner to the development of industry. Entrepreneurship is considered as a dynamic process of creating incremental wealth. This wealth is created by individuals who have been daring enough to undertake the major risks in terms of equity, time, and / or career commitment of providing value for some product or service. The product or service itself may not be unique or new but value must somehow be infused by the entrepreneur by securing and allocating these necessary skills and resources.

To understand an entrepreneur better, researchers have defined traits common to a majority of individuals who innovate and operate new ventures. Another way to explain entrepreneurship is from sociocultural stand point. In this method first hand information on entrepreneurs is collected through interviews which are usually conducted for data on socio-cultural aspects. Further data can be gathered through questionnaires on different functional aspects. These approaches usually defined the nature of entrepreneurship. Keeping some of these aspects in view a structured questionnaire for small entrepreneurs has been devised. This questionnaire has been administered to 150 small entrepreneurs operating industrial units in the North Telengana region i.e., Adilabad, Karimnagar, Khammam and Warangal districts of Telengana region in Andhra Pradesh. The questionnaire is divided into two sections. Section - A broadly covers the socio-economic profile of the respondents, while section - B deals specifically with the aspects assessing the managerial and other innovative aspects.

Socio-cultural Aspects of Entrepreneurs

The socio economic profile is mostly concerned with the sociocultural aspects of the entrepreneurs.

It is usually postulated that entrepreneurs gain by experience and hence the middle aged will have a higher proportion among the entrepreneurs than either youth or elderly people. The age of the entrepreneurs is shown in the Table 4.1.

Table 4.1
Age Distribution of Responders

Age (in years)	*Frequency*	*Percent*
Below 25	11	7.3
26-45	106	70.7
46-60	33	22.0
Total	150	100.0

Source: Field Survey

The age of entrepreneurs is divided into three groups; the first group representing those below 25 years, the second group in the age group of 26-45 years and those 45 years above in the third group. Those who are below 25 years have seven per cent in this total sample, while 71 per cent belong to the age group of 26-45 years. The remaining 22 per cent belong to 46-60 years age group. That the middle aged have a higher proportion among the entrepreneurs.

In the present world acquiring educational qualifications will be helpful for entrepreneurs, as most of them will be dealing with many other units for procuring raw materials and also to understand market trends for their product. The educational qualification of entrepreneurs has been shown in the table given below.

Table 4.2
Educational Qualifications of the Respondents

Educational qualification	*Frequency*	*Percent*
SSC	21	14.0
XII std	27	18.0
Graduation	71	47.3
Post-Graduation	31	20.7
Total	150	100.0

Source: Field Survey.

Among the entrepreneurs 14 per cent are educated up to SSC, 18 percent up to Intermediate 47.3 per cent up to graduate level and 20.7 per cent up to post-graduate level. Thus all the entrepreneurs are educated and a majority of them are graduates.

Table 4.3
Caste-wise Distribution of Entrepreneurs

Caste background	*Frequency*	*Percent*
Other castes	100	66.7
Backward classes	38	25.3
Scheduled Castes	09	6.0
Scheduled Tribes	03	2.0
Total	150	100.0

Source: Field Survey.

The caste of the entrepreneur gives an indication about the dominant caste group among the entrepreneurs. Though the government is making efforts to give encouragement to the weaker sections through entrepreneur development programmes to start new ventures, how far these efforts have been successful can be visuallised from Table 4.3.

Among the sample units, 66.7 per cent of the entrepreneurs belong to other castes, 25.3 per cent belong to backward castes, 6 per cent belong to scheduled caste and 2 per cent to scheduled tribes. It is evident from the caste wise breakup of the entrepreneurs that those who belong to other castes, that is upper castes, are in higher proposition signifying the dominance of this group among entrepreneurs operating small businesses.

Table 4.4
Number of Dependents in the Household

Number of Dependent	*Frequency*	*Percent*
0-3	08	05.3
4-7	49	32.7
8-11	77	21.3
11 and above	16	10.7
Total	150	100.0

Source: Field Survey.

The number of dependents in the household gives an idea about the nature of the household i.e. nuclear or joint. In the sample 5.3 per cent have 3 or less than 3 dependents, 32.7 per cent have dependents in the range of 4-7, 51.3 per cent have dependents in the range of 8-11, while 10. 7 per cent have more than 11 dependents. Thus the majority of the households have more than 8 dependents indicating that entrepreneurs have mostly originated from joint families.

The parent's occupation necessarily helps an entrepreneur to a certain extent, especially if the parents are also in the same line of production. Hence family background acquires some importance. This is shown in The table 4.5.

Table 4.5
Parent's Occupation of the Respondents

Parent's Occupation	*Frequency*	*Percent*
Government service	07	4.7
Private service	05	3.3
Agriculture	51	34.0
Business	75	50.0
Traditional family occupation	12	0.80
Total	150	100.0

Source: Field Survey.

Parent's occupation for 4% of entrepreneurs had been government service. In the case of 3.3% of entrepreneurs it had been private service. 34% of entrepreneurs hailed from agricultural families, while 50% have a business background. It is a traditional family occupation for 8 per cent. Thus those who have business as their family background are more prone to become entrepreneurs. The next occupation is those with agricultural background and these two occupations almost covered 85 per cent of sample units.

Whenever a new unit is established there would be some prime mover. The idea to start a unit must have occurred for the owner himself, or it could have been suggested by friends or relatives some times government agencies or financial institutions may also kindle interest for setting up of the unit. In the sample of 150 entrepreneurs 37 per cent have started the units of their own initiative and in the case of 14 per cent friends have given the idea; while in the case of 15 per cent relatives and government agencies played a catalytic role. In the remaining 19 per cent institutions are responsible floating the idea. Thus though self initiative had been responsible for the establishment of the units it is significant to note that the financial institutions and government agencies had also been motivating individuals to start the units.

In the present world, unlike in the past, some training is essential for an entrepreneur to become successful. In order to ascertain whether the entrepreneur received any vocational, technical or business training, a question has been put to them. Among the respondents, 72 per cent received such a training while 28 per cent did not receive any training. Thus a majority have some training before they started a unit, which signifies that entrepreneurial development programmes have achieved some success in motivating the entrepreneurs.

Table 4.6
Chi-square Test Homogeneity

Line of Production	*Cases observed*	*Cases expected*	*Residual*
Food processing	59	18.75	40.25
Engineering	07	18.75	11.75
Cement products	02	18.75	16.75
Cold storage/ Chemicals	06	18.75	-12.75
Plastics/ Polythene	06	18.75	-12.75
Animal food	01	18.75	-17.75
Granites	45	18.75	26.25
Roofing & Decorate tiles	24	18.75	5.25
Total	150		
	Chi-square 181.0933	D.F. 7	Significance .0000

Source: Field Survey.

The line of production in which the unit has been started ultimately decides whether the entrepreneur has taken a proper decision or otherwise. Among the various lines of production, food processing units have a prominent place as 39 per cent of the units have come under this group. The next line of production that had attracted a considerable number of entrepreneurs is granite industries, where 30 per cent of the entrepreneurs had invested their amount. Next in importance is roofing or decorative tiles with 16 per cent of the entrepreneurs in this line of production less than 5 per cent of the entrepreneurs can be found in other lines of production like engineering, cold storage, chemicals, plastics, cement products and animal food. Thus the major line of production for the sample units had been food processing, granites and tiles industries. The chi-square test for testing homogeneity postulated that is whether different lines of production can attract the same number of units, had been rejected at 5 per cent level of significance.

Table 4.7
Units Established in Different Years

Years of Establishment	*Frequency*	*Percent*
Before 1980	11	07.3
1985	16	10.7
1990	16	10.7
1995	61	40.7
After 1995	46	30.7
Total	150	100.0

Source: Field Survey.

The age of the unit indicates the length of the survival of the unit in a particular line of business. Data have been gathered on the year of establishment; before 1980, 7 per cent of the units were established; between 1980 and 1985 as well as 1985-90,

10.7 per cent units were initiated, between 1990-95, 40.7 per cent units were started and after 1995 the remaining units were started. Thus a majority of units were started after 1990 and so they are still a decade old. The units with a greater length of life constitute about one fourth of the total sample units.

Location, Organisational Aspects and Capital Structure of the Units

Table 4.8
Location of the Units in Different Districts

Name of Districts	*Frequency*	*Percent*
Adilabad	12	08.0
Karimnagar	20	13.3
Khammam	75	50.0
Warangal	43	28.7
Total	150	100.0

Source: Field Survey.

The location of a unit in a particular area has its advantages as financial and other infrastructural facilities which are required for setting up of such units may be available. Since the units established in four districts of North Telengana region of Andhra Pradesh were considered here the location factor is limited to the four districts in the region. The district-wise distribution of the sample units shows that 8% are located in Adilabad, 13.3% in Karimnagar, 50% in Khammam and 28.7% in Warangal. Thus Khammam has displayed a greater potential for entrepreneurs to set their units in that district, while Warangal comes next to Khammam. Adilabad is a very backward district which is in need of industrialisation, but it could not attract the entrepreneurs as only 8 per cent of the units had been established in that district.

Table 4.9
Form of the Organisation of the Units

Form of the Organisation	*Frequency*	*Percent*
Sole proprietor	90	60.0
Partnership	55	36.7
Joint-stock Company	05	03.3
Total	150	100.0

Source: Field Survey

Table 4.9(a)
Chi-Square Test of Homogeneity for the Organisation Form

Category	*Cases observed*	*Cases expected*	*Residual*
Sole proprietor	90	50.00	40.00
Partnership	55	50.00	5.00
Joint-Stock Company	05	50.00	-45.00
Total	150		
	Chi-square 73.00	D.F. 2	Significance .0000

Source: Field Survey.

The form of organisation of the units is equally important as the company form will favour large scale operation of the units. The form of the Organisation of the units indicates that 60 per cent are sole proprietorships, 36.7 per cent are under partnership and only 3.3 per cent of organisations are organised as joint stock companies. Thus there is a preponderance of sole proprietorship among the units. A chi-square test that the three types of industries have attracted the same number of units has been rejected at 5 per cent level of significance.

Table 4.10
Nature of the Goods Produced by the Units

Nature of the Goods	*Frequency*	*Percent*
Consumer Goods	101	67.3
Capital Goods	12	08.0
Intermediate Goods	37	24.7
Total	150	100.0

Source: Field Survey.

The type of the goods produced by the units is equally important, especially in the case of small units. The small units usually produce goods which can be marketed very easily within a short period of time. If that happens they can flourish well; otherwise, they run into difficulties as they may not be able to realise the investment on producing goods. In the case of small units 67.3 per cent produced exclusively consumer goods. The other type of goods is capital goods produced by 8 per cent of the units. There is production of intermediate goods by 24.7 per cent of the units. Thus a majority of the units are specialising in the production of consumer goods.

Table 4.11
Shifts Operated by the Units

No. of Shifts for Units	*Frequency*	*Percent*
One shift	26	17.3
Two Shifts	75	50.0
Three Shifts	49	32.7
Total	150	100.0

Source: Field Survey.

The number of shifts operated by a unit reflects the performance of the units. If the products of the units are in great demand, the production units could be running two/three shifts for day. In the case of sample units also such a phenomenon can be observed; out of the 150 sample units 17.3 per cent of the units are running for one shift; 50 per cent of the units are running for two shifts and 32.7 per cent for three shifts. Thus a considerable majority of the units are running for more than one shift. Hence 83 per cent of the units are utilising their plant and machinery for two or three shifts per day to meet the demand for their products in the market, which also reflects that they are moderately successful in running their units.

Table 4.12
Installed Capacity of the Units

Installed capacity (in lakhs of Rs.)	*Frequency*	*Percent*
Below 25	59	39.3
25-50	67	44.7
50-75	20	13.3
75 and above	04	02.7
Total	150	100.0

Source: Field Survey.

Table 4.12(a)
Chi-Square Test of Homogeneity for Installed Capacity

Installed Capacity (in lakhs of Rs.)	*Cases observed*	*Cases expected*	*Residual*
below 25	59	37.50	21.50
25-50	67	37.50	29.50
50-75	20	37.50	-17.50
75 & above	04	37.50	-33.50
Total	150		
	Chi-square 73.6267	D.F. 3	Significance .0000

Source: Field Survey.

The installed capacity of the unit is equally important in the production plans of the units. As the installed capacity is in quantitative terms and varies from one unit to another unit, the capacity is shown as lakhs of rupees invested by the firm as on 31-3-1998. In the case of the sample units, 39.3 per cent of the units have Rs. 25 Lakh or below as installed capacity; in the case of 44.7 per cent of the units the installed capacity is in the range of 25-50 lakhs. In the case of 30.3% of the units the installed capacity ranges between Rs. 50-75 lakh and in the case of 2.7 per cent of the units the value of the installed capacity is more than Rs. 75 lakh. A chi-square test for testing the equality of installed capacity among the units classified according to their capital structure shows that the hypothesis is rejected at 5 per cent level of significance.

Table 4.13
No. of Workers in a Unit

No. of Workers per unit	*Frequency*	*Percent*
Below 5	02	01.3
6-10	10	06.7
11-20	62	41.3
Above 20	76	50.7
Total	150	100.0

Source: Field Survey.

The size of the employment generated by the industrial units is important in view of the SSI sector's role in employment generation in the society. Among 150 units 1.3 per cent of the units are employing below 5 workers, in the case of 6.7 per cent of the units the employment is between 6-10 workers per unit. Likewise for 41.3 per cent of the units the range of employment is between 11-20 and for 50.7 per cent of the units employment is about 20 workers per unit. Thus a majority of the units that is almost 90 per cent of the units, employ more than 10 workers, signifying that they could generate employment to a certain extent.

Table 4.14
Percentage of the Actual Days Functioned by the Units

No. of Actual days Per annum (in %)	*Frequency*	*Percent*
Below 25	01	00.7
25-50	29	19.3
50-75	80	53.3
Above 75	40	26.7
Total	150	100.0

Source: Field Survey.

The percentage of actual days worked per annum is an indicator of the manner in which the small scale units are functioning. The greater the percentage, one can conclude that they are functioning in a better manner. Among the sample units only 0.7 per cent of the units have below 25 per cent of 365 days per annum as the actual days in which the units has been functioning in the case of 90.3 per cent, 53.3 per cent and 26.7 per cent of the units the actual days of the working per annum was found to be in the ranges of 25-50 per cent, 50-75 per cent and above 75 per cent respectively. Thus a majority of the units are functioning for at least 6 months in a year.

Every industrial unit requires investments in fixed capital as well as working capital. The investment in fixed capital by the sample units is shown in Table 4.15.

Table 4.15
Investment in Fixed Capital by the Sample Units

Fixed Capital (in lakhs of Rs.)	*Frequency*	*Percent*
Below 5	15	10.0
5-15	38	25.3
15-25	53	35.3
25-50	30	20.0
Above 50	14	09.3
Total	150	100.0

Source: Field Survey.

Table 4.15(a)
Chi-Square Test of Homogeneity for Fixed Capital

Fixed Capital (in lakhs of Rs.)	*Cases observed*	*Cases expected*	*Residual*
Below 5	15	30.00	-15.00
5-15	38	30.00	8.00
15-25	53	30.00	23.00
25-50	14	30.00	0.00
Above 50	14	30.00	-16.00
Total	150		
	Chi-square 35.8000	D.F. 4	Significance .0000

Source: Field Survey.

Out of all the units 10 per cent have Rs. 5 lakh or lesser than that as the investment in fixed capital. In the range of Rs. 6-15 lakh investment in fixed capital has been done by 25.3 per cent of the units. In the case of 35.5 per cent of the units fixed capital is in the range of Rs. 16-25 lakh. In the interval of Rs. 26-50 lakh, 20 per cent of the sample units have invested in fixed capital. Investment in fixed capital crossing Rs. 50 lakh can be observed in the case 4 units whose investment in fixed capital has crossed even one crore of rupees. Thus we find a majority of the units having their fixed capital investment being less than Rs. 25 lakh, which indicates that over time the fixed capital requirements had gone up considerably, when compared with their requirements in the earlier decades. A chi-square test for testing the hypothesis whether the number units are same in all the 5 different capital structures. The hypothesis was rejected at 5 per cent level of significance.

The small scale units often have more working capital requirements. In certain consumer goods industries the working capital requirements would be more than the fixed capital requirements. The Table 4.16 shows the working capital requirements of the sample units. Out of the 150 units 9.3 per cent of the units are investing less than Rs. 5 lakhs as their working capital. Here a similarity can be observed where about 10 per cent of the total units have also less than Rs. 5 lakh as their fixed capital investment. A considerable percentage of the units are investing in the range of Rs. 6-15 lakh as the working capital indicating that some of the units which are having a higher fixed capital requirements, for instance those in the range of Rs. 16-25 lakh are also having working capital requirements below Rs. 15 lakh. In the other ranges that is Rs. 16-25 lakh, Rs. 26-50 lakh, we find 18 per cent, 16.7 per cent of the units having their working capital requirements respectively.

Table 4.16
Investment in Working Capital by the Sample Units

Working Capital (in lakhs of Rs.)	*Frequency*	*Percent*
Below 5	14	09.3
5-15	66	44.0
15-25	27	18.0
25-50	25	16.7
Above 50	18	12.0
Total	150	100.0

Source: Field Survey.

All the 9.3 per cent of the total units that are investing more than Rs. 50 lakh in fixed capital are having higher working capital requirements and are included in the 12 per cent of the units that are having their working capital requirements well above Rs. 50 lakh which is indicative that some of the units having less than Rs. 50 lakh investment in fixed capital are also having higher requirements of working capital.

In the case of the small units institutional finance has an

important role, as it becomes imperative for these units may not be able to procure their complete capital requirements from non-institutional sources. Further there are certain financial institutions like APSFC, SIDCO, NCIS, which are extending financial help for the small scale Units.

Table 4.17
Institutional Finance for the Sample Units

Institutional Finance (in %)	*Frequency*	*Percent*
Not receiving finance	48	32.0
Below 5	09	06.0
5-10	52	34.7
10-15	23	15.3
15-20	11	07.3
20-25	07	04.7
Total	150	100.0

Source: Field Survey.

Out of the total sample units 32 per cent are not depending on institutional finance. In the case of 6 per cent of the units only less than 5 per cent of the requirements are being met by institutional finance. In the case of 8 % of the units below 10 per cent of their requirements are financed through institutions; for 34.7 per cent of the units, below 15 per cent; for 15.3 per cent of the units, below 20 per cent for 7.3 per cent of the units below 25% for 4.7% of the units. Thus in a majority of the cases the institutional finance is able to meet less than 15% of their financial requirements and no unit is getting financial help for more than 25 per cent of the total financial requirements. These findings exemplify the dwindling need for institutional finance even in the case of SSI units.

Table 4.18
Sources of Finance for Fixed Capital Requirements

Name of the Institution	*Frequency*	*Percent*
SIDCO	76	50.7
NSIC	09	06.0
APSFC	19	19.3
Equity Capital	11	07.3
Pvt. Finance	25	16.7
Total	150	100.0

Source: Field Survey.

Table 4.19
Type of Loans from Institutional Non-Institutional Sources for the Sample Units

Type of Loan	*Frequency*	*Percent*
Cash Credit	30	20.0
Over draft	10	06.7
Demand Loans	13	08.7
Term Loans	57	38.0
Equity	14	09.3
Pvt. Finance	26	17.3
Total	150	100.0

Source: Field Survey.

The capital requirements as per the finances advanced through certain institutions indicate the number of units depending on the two types of financial sources. Out of the total units, 15.7 per cent of the units had received financial help from SIDCO, but SIC and APSFC had been financing 6 per cent and 19.3 per cent of the units respectively. Raising fixed capital through equity is also resorted to by these small scale units and in case of 7.3 per cent of the units equity capital is being raised from capital market. Lastly 16.3 per cent of the units are depending on private finance. Thus among all the institutional as well as non-institutional sources in a majority of the cases the institutional finance is the source and for about 50 per cent of the units it is SIDCO which is financing their requirements. The SSI units depend on institutional finance for their working capital requirements. The units can try to raise the finance required for working capital in different modes from the financial institutions.

Table 4.19(a)

Chi-square Test of Homogeneity of Different Categories of Financing

Categories of Financing	*Cases observed*	*Cases expected*	*Residual*
Cash credit	3.0	25.0	5.00
Over draft	1.0	25.0	-15.00
Demand loans	1.3	25.0	-12.00
Term Loans	5.7	25.0	32.00
Equity	1.4	25.0	-11.00
Pvt. Finance	26	25.00	1.00
Total	150		
	Chi-square 61.6000	D.F. 5	Significance .0000

Source: Field Survey.

Among all the sample units cash credit is a form of financing for 20 per cent of the units, over draft facilities have been used by 6.7 per cent of the units, but most of the units use demand loans or term loans for their working capital requirements. Among these units, 8.7 per cent are raising demand loans and 38 per cent of the units are raising their requirements in the shape of term loans. Equity capital and private finance are meeting the financial needs of 9.3 per cent and 17.3 per cent of the units respectively. Hence a considerable number of units are meeting their working capital requirements either through term loans or cash credit. Another significant finding is that in the case of working capital requirements about 75 per cent of the units are depending on institutional finance. The type of credit under which they are prompted to borrow for working capital has the same number of firms under each category has been tested with the help of the chi-square test and the hypothesis had been rejected at 5 per cent level of significance.

Table 4.20

Gap between Working Capital Requirements and Actual Capital Available

Gap in the Working Capital Requirement (in lakhs of Rs.)	*Frequency*	*Percent*
Below 5	39	26.0
05-10	54	36.0
10-15	20	13.3
15-25	15	10.0
25-50	22	14.7
Total	150	100.0

Source: Field Survey.

Table 4.20(a)

Chi-Square Test of Homogeneity in Case of Working Capital Requirements

Gap in the Working Capital Requirement	*Cases observed*	*Cases expected*	*Residual*
Below 5	3.9	30.0	9.00
05-10	54	30.0	24.00
10-15	20	30.0	-10.00
15-25	1.5	30.0	-15.00
25-50	22	30.0	-8.00
Total	150		
	Chi-square	D.F.	Significance
	34.8667	4	.0000

Source: Field Survey.

In many of the small scale units the working capital requirements of the units, which naturally depend on the size of the unit, may be more than the amount they could procure towards working capital. Thus there exists a gap between their actual requirements and the amount invested by them. An analysis of gap shows that 26 per cent of the total units are short of their capital to the tune of less than Rs. 5 lakh; in case of 36 per cent of the units the range is in between Rs. 6-10 lakhs. Likewise 13.3 per cent, 10 per cent and 14.7 per cent of the units have their gaps in the ranges of Rs. 11-15 lakh, Rs. 16-25 lakh and Rs. 25-50 lakh respectively. Thus a majority of the firms are experiencing capital crunch to the extent of Rs. 10 lakh or less than that amount and it is significant to note that no single firm is able to raise their required amount for working capital from the financial markets. Thus there is a need for more capital for investment purposes and the persistence of this gap may not be conducive for the progress of the small units. A chi-square test had been conducted for a hypothesis that the number of firms under each class interval is the same and it has been rejected at 5 per cent level of significance.

Thus this analysis shows that a majority of entrepreneurs are middle aged and studied up to graduate level. They mostly belong to upper castes having a business background. The units have been set up mostly on the initiative of the entrepreneurs themselves and the frequency of entrepreneurs is to either setup a unit in food processing line of production or granites. Most of the units are of recent origin. Most of the entrepreneurs received some training before they started a unit sole proprietorship in the dominant form of business organisation and most of them are producing consumer goods. A majority of the firms are operating either two shifts or three shifts and the value of the installed capacity is more than Rs. 25 lakh for three fifty of the units. A majority of the units employ more than 10 workers and normally they work for more than six months. The value of fixed capital invested by the units who that about two thirds of the units have invested more than Rs. 15 lakh, but the working capital requirements are for more than

Rs. 50 lakh in the case of some firms which have fixed capital in the same range. Institutional finance is being provided for two thirds of the units and three fifths of the units depend for more than 50% of their finance on institutional finance. Among the institutions providing financial assistance, SIDCO has a higher share than other institutions. Term loans are usually borrowed by the units, though overdraft and other forms of credit are also being utilized by the firms are experiency a capital crunch for further expansion of the capacity utilization of the firms.

5
Entrepreneurial Aspects of the Firms – Some Findings

Entrepreneurship has a major role in the efficient functioning of a firm, certain parameters that are often employed to assess efficiency of the firm are:

i) Whether the firm is modernizing its equipment;

ii) Whether there had been an expansion of the capacity of the firm;

iii) The ingenuity in tapping the financial sources;

iv) The growth pattern of the sales of the firm;

v) The principal markets of the firm;

vi) The utilization of export promotion measures to help the opportunities in the international market; and

vii) The profitability of a firm.

Some of these aspects have been analyzed here by eliciting responses from the entrepreneurs.

Entrepreneurs' Views on the Expansion of Capacity and Modernization

Replacement of old machinery by new machinery is one of the indications whether entrepreneurs are using modern

Table 5.1
Views on Replacement of Machinery as Per Capital Structure of the Firms

(in Rs. Lakhs)

Response	*Investment in Capital (in lakhs of Rupees)*											
	Below 5		*5 -15*		*15-25*		*25-50*		*above 50*		*Total*	
	Fixed capital	*Working capital*	*Fixed capital*	*Working capital*	*Fixed capital*	*Working capital*	*Fixed capital*	*Working capital*	*Fixed capital*	*Working capital*	*Fixed capital*	*Working capital*
Yes	12.0	9.0	18.0	30.0	28.0	20.0	25.0	22.0	10.0	12.0	93.0 (62.0)	93.0 (62.0)
No	3.0	5.0	20.0	36.0	25.0	7.0	5.0	3.0	4.0	6.0	57.0 (38.0)	57.0 (38.0)
Total	15.0 (10.0)	14.0 (9.3)	38.0 (25.3)	66.0 (44.0)	53.0 (35.3)	27.0 (18.0)	30.0 (20.0)	25.0 (16.7)	14.0 (9.3)	18.0 (12.0)	150.0 (100.0)	150.0 (100.0)

Note: Figures in parentheses are row percentage.

machinery or they are increasing the capacity of the units. Table 5.1 shows the respondents' views on this aspect.

To a question whether they have replaced the machinery in the last 5 years, 62 per cent have said yes and the remaining no. Since the responses vary according to the capital structure of the firm, the analysis had been carried out in terms of the fixed and working capital structure. In the case of those having Rs. 5 lakhs or below as their fixed capital, 80 per cent have said that they have replaced their machinery; while in the case of those having Rs. 5-15 lakh, 44 per cent have said in the affirmative while the remaining said no. In the case of Rs. 15-25 lakh, Rs. 25-50 lakh and above Rs. 50 lakh, a higher percentage among the entrepreneurs had replied that they had replaced the machinery. This type of replacement is to be observed in higher proportion in the case of firms having more than Rs. 25 lakh as their fixed capital. Thus the units in considerable number which could not replace machinery are to be found among the units having their fixed capital in the range of Rs. 5-25 lakh. When the replacement aspects are considered from the working capital invested by the firms, once again firms investing in the range of Rs. 5-15 lakh as working capital have more number of firms not replacing the machinery.

Table 5.2
Respondents' Views on Replacement of Machinery on the basis of their Education

Response	*Educational Qualifications*				
	SSC	*XII std*	*Degree*	*P.G.*	*Total*
Yes	17	22	39	15	93 (62.0)
No	04	05	32	16	57 (38.0)
Total	21 (14.0)	27 (18.0)	71 (47.3)	31 (20.7)	150 (100.0)

Note: Figures in parentheses are row percentage.

Thus both in the case of the fixed capital as well as working capital the firms operating in the range of Rs. 5-15 lakh a sizeable number could not replace their machinery.

To what extent educational qualifications or caste can influence the decision to replace the machinery had also been examined here. It is often assumed that higher educational qualifications may have some influence on entrepreneurs decision to replace the machinery. Replacement of machinery had been undertaken by entrepreneurs who are all undergraduates, while in the case of graduates the number of those who replaced the machinery is likely to be higher than those who did not, the proportion of those who replaced the machinery is much higher in the case of less educated entrepreneurs. In the case of those who did their post graduation, a number of them replaced their machinery. This analysis indicates that higher educational attainment need not lead to an entrepreneur replacing their machinery or they try to modernize their firms.

Table 5.3
Respondents' Views on Replacement of Machinery (Caste-wise)

Response	*Caste Background*				
	OC	*BC*	*SC*	*ST*	*Total*
Yes	74	12	04	03	93 (62.0)
No	45	10	02	-	57 (38.0)
Total	119 (79.3)	22 (14.7)	06 (4.0)	3· (2.0)	150 (100.0)

Note: Figures in parentheses are row percentage.

It is usually presumed that caste differences may also contribute to decision making and when decision to replace the machinery has been examined on the basis of the category of the entrepreneur, in all the castes those who had replaced the machinery were higher in number than those who did not. But the difference between those who said yes and those who said no is much in the case of BC's and in the case of ST's all have replaced their machinery. Thus some castes are more enthusiastic in replacing the machinery than the other caste groups.

When machinery is being replaced, some sort of financing required among those who said yes, 8.7 per cent of the respondent has replied that they would utilize the internal surplus generated by their units. A considerable number said that they approached various institutions, primarily banks for financing their requirements; only 1 per cent depended on private finance. Thus the higher percentage of respondents depended on institutional finance and contrary to the usual hypothesis that internal surplus plays a major role in the modernization process, it is institutional finance that is playing an important role in these units.

Table 5.4

Castewise Response on the Expansion of Capacity in the Last Five Years

Response	*Caste Background*				
	OC	*BC*	*SC*	*ST*	*Total*
Yes	80	14	04	03	101 (67.3)
No	39	08	02	-	49 (32.7)
Total	119 (79.3)	22 (14.7)	06 (4.0)	3 (2.0)	150 (100.0)

Note: Figures in parentheses are row percentage.

To another question whether there had been an expansion in the capacity of the unit during the last 5 years, 67.3 per cent have said yes, while the remaining did not expand their capacity. All the ST's in the samples have expanded their capacity, while among SC's 67.00 per cent have done so. Among

Table 5.5

Responses Regarding Expansion of Units on the basis of Profits Earned by the Firms in 1995-96,1996-97 & 1997-98

Response	*Profits (in thousands of Rs.)*								
	0 - 5			*5 - 10*			*10 - 20*		
	1995-96	*1996-67*	*1997-98*	*1995-96*	*1996-67*	*1997-98*	*1995-96*	*1996-67*	*1997-98*
Yes	14	10	3	21	22	30	47	44	31
No	13	8	1	12	12	16	18	23	16
Total	27 (18.0)	18 (12.0)	4 (2.7)	33 (27.0)	34 (22.7)	46 (30.7)	65 (43.3)	67 (44.7)	47 (31.3)

20-25			*25 - 50*			*50 & above*			*Total*		
1995-96	*1996-67*	*1997-98*	*1995-96*	*1996-67*	*1997-98*	*1995-96*	*1996-67*	*1997-98*	*1995-96*	*1996-67*	*1997-98*
13	16	17	3	4	11	3	5	9	101 (67.3)	101 (67.3)	101 (67.3)
6	6	14	-	-	2	-	-	-	49 (32.7)	49 (32.7)	49 (32.7)
19 (12.7)	22 (14.7)	31 (20.7)	3 (2.0)	4 (2.7)	13 (8.7)	3 (2.0)	5 (3.0)	9 (6.0)	150 (100.0)	150 (100.0)	150 (100.0)

Note: Figures in parentheses are row percentage.

BC's about 65 per cent have expanded the capacity while in the case of OC's 75 per cent have expanded their capacity. Thus caste wise configuration shows that ST's and OC's have a relative higher percentage than ST's and BC's in undertaking the expansion of the capacity.

Table 5.6
Expansion of the Units through Various Forms of Finance

Percentage of the Finance from a Source	*Internal surplus*		*Institutional finance*		*Pvt. Finance*	
	Frequency	*Percent*	*Frequency*	*Percent*	*Frequency*	*Percent*
Nil	53	35.3	48	32.0	52	34.7
Below 5	49	27.7	09	06.0	24	16.0
5-10	26	17.3	52	34.7	20	13.3
10-15	07	04.7	23	15.3	32	21.3
15-25	09	06.0	11	07.3	12	08.0
Above 25	06	04.0	07	04.7	10	6.7
Total	150	100.0	150	100.0	150	100.0

Note: Figures in parentheses are row percentage.

Earning profits is an indication whether a firm is essentially successful or not and the expansion of capacity depends on the capacity of a firm to earn more profits. Hence in the above table, the decision to expand has been examined vis-à-vis the profit making capacity of the units. In 1995-96, among the units which could earn profits a considerable number had gone for expansion, but this number is almost same to that of those which did not expand. In the subsequent years the number of loss making units had declined and the tendency of a relatively higher number trying to expand their capacity is evident in the other two years also. In the case of the units earning less than Rs. 5,000 profits, the number of units making profits in this range had been slowly increasing in all the years. The tendency is for more firms trying to expand the capacity; for instance

Table 5.7

Units Planning Expansion in the Next Two Years based on their Capital Structure *(in Lakhs of Rs.)*

Response	*Below 5*		*5-15*		*15-25*		*25-50*		*above 50*		*Total*	
	Fixed capital	*Working capital*	*Fixed capital*	*Working capital*	*Fixed capital*	*Working capital*	*Fixed capital*	*Working capital*	*Fixed capital*	*Working capital*	*Fixed capital*	*Working capital*
Yes	5	9	13	27	28	10	18	15	10	13	74 (49.3)	74 (49.3)
No	10	5	25	39	25	17	12	10	4	5	76 (50.7)	76 (50.7)
Total	15 (10.0)	14 (9.3)	38 (25.3)	66 (44.0)	53 (35.3)	27 (18.0)	30 (20.0)	25 (16.7)	14 (9.3)	18 (12.0)	150 (100.0)	150 (100.0)

Note: Figures in parentheses are row percentage.

even in the case of other class intervals for profit earning like Rs. 5-10 thousand, Rs. 10-20 thousand, the tendency for the units expanding their capacity is more pronounced in a greater number. In the case of the firms earning profits either in Rs. 20-25 thousand range or in the range of Rs. 25-50 thousand or Rs. 50 thousand and above. All the units have undertaken expansion in 1995-96 and 1996-97. Thus units which are making profits in the higher range had generally gone for expansion of capacity in the last 5 years.

Table 5.8
Units Planning Expansion on the Basis of the Profits Earned by them in 1995-96

(in Thousands of Rs.)

	Earning of Profits						
Response	*0-5*	*5-10*	*10-15*	*15-20*	*20-25*	*25 & above*	*Total*
Yes	22	13	26	9	3	1	74 (49.3)
No	5	20	39	10	-	2	76 (50.7)
Total	27 (18.0)	33 (22.0)	65 (43.3)	19 (12.7)	3 (2.0)	3 (2.0)	150 (100.0)

Note: Figures in parentheses are row percentage.

Among those who said that they had expanded their capacity in the last 5 years, this expansion had been mainly facilitated by either internal surplus or institutional finance. Internal surplus had been utilized by about two-thirds of the sample units. Among these units, there is a variation in the utilization of internal surplus of all the units 32.7 per cent had utilized only less than 5 per cent of the internal surplus for expansion of capacity; likewise 17.3 per cent utilized less than 10 per cent; 4.7 per cent utilizing less than 15 per cent; 6 per cent utilizing in the interval of 15-25 per cent and finally 4 per cent of the units utilizing above 25 per cent of their internal surplus. Thus a relatively higher proportion of the units are utilizing less than 10 per cent of their internal surplus for expanding their capacity.

Some of the units approached various institutions, especially the units expanding their capacity. As in the case of firms not utilizing internal surplus, here also 32 per cent of the units have not utilized institutional finance; a small percentage i.e., 6 per cent depended on institutional finance for less than 5 per cent of their financial requirements; in the case of 34.7 per cent, 15.3 per cent, 7.3 per cent and 4.7 per cent of the total units the institutional finance could meet the financial requirements for expanding their capacity in the ranges of 10-15 per cent, 15-25 per cent and above 25 per cent respectively. Here a considerable number can be found to depend for more than 10 per cent of their requirements on institutional finance for expanding their capacity.

Out of the total units, 34.7 per cent are not utilizing private finance, of the remaining 65.3 per cent of the units utilizing private finance, 16 per cent are utilizing private finance to the extent of less than 5 per cent of their total financial requirements. Likewise in the ranges of 5-10 per cent, 10-15 per cent, 15-25 per cent and above 25 per cent we find 13.3 per cent, 21.3 per cent, 8.0 per cent and 6.7 per cent of the units utilizing private finance respectively. Thus we find more than one third of the total units depending on private finance for 15 per cent of their capital requirements.

One of the important aspects of the entrepreneurship is planning for future. Hence a question has been asked whether the units are going to replace the machinery in the coming 2 years, if they had not already replaced, and at the same time whether they are planning for expansion if they had not already done it. In the total sample those who said that they are not planning either replacement or expansion of plants machinery in the next 2 years constitute 50.7 per cent of the sample and those who are planning for either replacement or expansion from 49.3 per cent of the sample. Thus in the case of those who said no, one reason is that a majority of the entrepreneurs had either replaced their machinery or expanded their units in the last 5 years; hence response for this question is muted. Thus this finding shows units would expand only in certain favourable conditions and it depends on the assessment of the conditions by the entrepreneurs and there could be certain differences between units that invested lesser capital and units that invested more capital. Therefore the capital structure of the industries was also taken into consideration in analyzing responses.

Among the units that invested less than Rs. 5 lakh in fixed capital or those that invested in the range or Rs. 5-15 lakh two-thirds or more than two-thirds of units are not planning either replacement or expansion in the next 2 years. In the case of units that invested in the range of Rs. 15-25 lakh those units planning for expansion is more. The gap between those who said yes and those who said no is small but in the higher ranges of investment that is Rs. 25-50 lakh or above 50 lakh those who said yes are considerable in number and the gap between those who said yes and those who said no is also relatively high. Thus as the investment of the units increases, the entrepreneurs are willing to either replace the machinery or plan expansion of their unit in the near future.

Besides the investment in fixed capital, investment in working capital can also be an indicator for the decision of the entrepreneurs to expand their units. Those entrepreneurs who invest more in working capital are prone for either replacement of the machinery or expansion of the units.

Among the units there is a peculiar tendency; that is units less than Rs. 5 lakhs or more than Rs. 25 lakh in working capital are planning for expansion in future. But a majority of the units operating with working capital in the ranges of Rs. 5-15 lakh and Rs. 15-25 lakh are not planning for either replacement of machinery or expansion of the units. Hence working capital requirement also had a constraint for expansion among units investing in the lower capital ranges.

The profits earned in a recent year can also influence the decision regarding replacement of machinery or expansion of the units. Here also units operating with profits less than Rs. 5,000 or more than Rs. 25,000 are willing to expand their firms. Among the units earning profits in the range of Rs.10-15 thousands a higher percentage are willing to expand their firms. Thus very low profit earned and very high profit earned in a relative sense can take the decision to expand their firms in the next 2 years.

Entrepreneurs have to raise finances in the capital market and in most of the cases it is presumed that they approach institutions for raising adequate finance either for replacement of machinery or for expansion of the units as they could be caste-wise differences. The manner in which finances has been raised for future expansion of units is shown in Table 5.9.

Table 5.9
Proposed Sources of Finance for Expansion of the Units in Next Two Years

Percentage of the Finance from a Source	*Internal surplus*		*Institutional finance*		*Pvt. Finance*	
	Frequency	*Percent*	*Frequency*	*Percent*	*Frequency*	*Percent*
Nil	76	50.7	74	47.3	72	48.0
Below 5	37	24.7	5	3.3	23	15.3
5-10	17	11.3	22	14.7	19	12.7
10-15	08	5.3	23	15.3	12	8.0
15-25	07	4.7	9	6.0	14	9.3
Above 25	05	3.3	17	11.3	10	6.7
Total	150	100.0	150	100.0	150	100.0

Note: Figures in parentheses are row percentage.

Among the different sources of finance to be utilized by the units in the next two years for the expansion of the firms, three sources namely internal surplus, institutional finance and private finance had been mentioned. Among those who said

Table 5.10
Castewise Break - up for the Utilisation of Different Sources of Finance

Response	Other Castes			Backward Castes			Scheduled Castes			Scheduled Tribes			Total		
	Internal Surplus	*Institutional finance*	*Pvt. Finance*	*Internal Surplus*	*Institutional finance*	*Pvt. Finance*	*Internal Surplus*	*Institutional finance*	*Pvt. Finance*	*Internal Surplus*	*Institutional finance*	*Pvt. Finance*	*Internal Surplus*	*Institutional finance*	*Pvt. Finance*
Nil	63	62	61	10	9	8	2	2	2	1	1	1	76 (50.7)	74 (49.3)	72 (48.0)
Below 5	28	3	19	5	2	1	3	-	2	1	-	1	37 (24.7)	5 (3.3)	23 (15.3)
5-10	15	18	10	1	3	7	-	1	1	1	-	1	17 (11.3)	22 (14.7)	19 (12.7)
10-15	6	17	11	1	3	1	1	1	-	-	2	-	8 (5.3)	23 (15.3)	12 (8.0)
15-25	5	4	10	2	4	4	-	1	-	-	-	-	7 (4.7)	9 (6.0)	14 (9.3)
Above 25	2	15	8	3	1	1	-	1	1	-	-	-	5 (3.3)	17 (11.3)	10 (6.7)
Total	119 (79.3)	119 (79.3)	119 (79.3)	22 (14.7)	22 (14.7)	22 (14.7)	6 (4.0)	6 (4.0)	6 (4.0)	3 (2.0)	3 (2.0)	3 (2.0)	150 (100.0)	150 (100.0)	150 (100.0)

Note: Figures in parentheses are row percentage and column percentage.

they are using internal surplus, 24.7 per cent are utilizing less than 5 per cent in the range of 5-10, 10-15, 15-25 we find 11.3 per cent, 5.3 per cent and 4.7 per cent of the units utilizing this source. Only 3.3 per cent of the units are depending for more than 25 per cent of their financial requirements on internal surplus. In the case of institutional finance, a few are utilizing less than 5 per cent, but we find relatively higher percentage of units utilizing this source in the other ranges namely 5-10 per cent, 10-15 per cent, 15-25 per cent. Even in the case of units depending for more than 25 per cent financial requirements, we find 11.3 per cent of the units. Among those units utilizing private finance, a relatively higher percentage, that is 15.3 per cent are depending for less than 5 per cent on their financial requirements. Thus we find a considerable number of units will be depending on institutional finance.

Caste-wise considerations show that a considerable number among OC's and BC's could meet their financial requirements to the extent of 5 per cent or less than 5 per cent from their internal surplus but in the case of those who are using internal surplus for 10 per cent of their requirement, the number is more for OC's category than other caste categories; in the higher range of 25 per cent one SC is utilizing internal surplus, while one ST is utilizing internal surplus for 15 per cent of the requirements. Only in the case of two OC's, three BC's more than 25 per cent of their financial requirements are being met from their internal surplus. In the case of caste-wise utilization of institutional finance, especially bank finance is examined, here also about 50 per cent are depending for less than 5 per cent of their requirements on institutional finance; at the other extreme, more than 25 per cent of their requirements are being met in the case of 15 units of OC's, and one unit each in the case of BC and SC. In the case of 4 OC's and 4 BC's the institutional finance is in the range of 15-25 per cent of the requirements. In the case of SC's except for two all others are depending for 15 per cent or more of their requirements on institutional finance. In the case of ST's, two respondents are utilizing the institutional financing for above 15 per cent of their requirements. The third source, private finance is required for less than 5 per cent in the case of 48 per cent of the respondents only 6.7 per cent of the respondents are depending on private finance for more than 25 per cent of their financial requirements.

Table 5.11
Adequate Finance from the Financial Institutions

Repsonse	*Other Castes*	*Backward Classes*	*Scheduled Castes*	*Scheduled Tribes*	*Total*
YES	88	20	04	2	114 (76.0)
NO	31	2	2	1	36 (24.0)
TOTAL	119 (79.3)	22 (14.7)	6 (4.0)	3 (2.0)	150 (100.0)

Note: Figures in parentheses are row percentage.

Adequacy of finances from financial institutions is essential for maintaining the scale of operations by each individual unit. A question has been put about the adequacy of finance to the respondents. Among the respondents; 76 per cent said that it is adequate. Caste-wise differences show that more than two-thirds of the respondents under each caste are satisfied with the provision of finances from institution. The responses show that among different castes BC's have felt mostly that the institutional finance had been adequate when compared with other castes.

In the case of bank finance there are instances where banks tried to supply the finance without taking into cognizance the needs for the entrepreneurs. Hence a question had been put whether the finance had been provided to the entrepreneurs at the proper time. Among the 150 respondents 66 per cent have said that the bank finance was given according to their requirements while the remaining said that they could not get the finance at the needed hour. Among those who said bank finance was given at the proper time a majority belong to those

Table 5.12
Respondents' Views on Need-based Finance from Banks based on the Capital Structure of the Units

(in Lakhs of Rs.)

Response	*Below 5*		*5 -15*		*15-25*		*25-50*		*above 50*		*Total*	
	Fixed capital	*Working capital*	*Fixed capital*	*Working capital*	*Fixed capital*	*Working capital*	*Fixed capital*	*Working capital*	*Fixed capital*	*Working capital*	*Fixed capital*	*Working capital*
Yes	13	12	21	46	37	15	19	14	9	12	99 (66.0)	99 (66.0)
No	2	2	17	20	16	12	11	11	5	6	51 (34.0)	51 (34.0)
Total	15 (10.0)	14 (9.3)	38 (25.3)	66 (44.0)	53 (35.3)	27 (18.0)	30 (20.0)	25 (16.7)	14 (9.3)	18 (12.0)	150 (100.0)	150 (100.0)

Note: Figures in parentheses are row percentage.

Table 5.13
Assistance from Financial Institutions *(in Lakhs of Rs.)*

Nursing the accounts by financial institution	Below 5		5 -15		15-25		25-50		above 50		Total	
	Fixed capital	*Working capital*	*Fixed capital*	*Working capital*	*Fixed capital*	*Working capital*	*Fixed capital*	*Working capital*	*Fixed capital*	*Working capital*	*Fixed capital*	*Working capital*
Yes	10	7	9	23	18	9	10	5	5	8	52 (34.7)	52 (34.7)
No	5	7	29	43	35	18	20	20	9	10	98 (65.3)	98 (65.3)
Total	15 (10.0)	14 (9.3)	38 (25.3)	66 . (44.0)	53 (35.3)	27 (18.0)	30 (20.0)	25 (16.7)	14 (9.3)	18 (12.0)	150 (100.0)	150 (100.0)

Note: Figures in parentheses are row percentage.

who were investing in the range of Rs. 5-15 lakh as their working capital and Rs. 15-25 lakh in case of fixed capital, but in the case of units which are investing in higher ranges either in the case of fixed capital of working capital the gap between those who said yes and those who said no is more in the case of the above Rs. 50 lakh group, indicating that this group could get adequate finance from institutions especially banks.

When institutions advance amounts to the small scale units they often monitor the loans. For this purpose the institution may provide special service or assistance to the units, usually these service could be in the form of nursing the account, providing advice on financial aspects or advice on marketing/ purchase or other aspects.

Table 5.13(a)
Assistance from Financial Institutions as per Respondent's Family Background

Nursing the accounts by financial institutions	*Govt. Service*	*Pvt.*	*Agri-culture*	*Business family*	*Traditional Service*	*Total*
Yes	4	-	21	24	3	52 (34.7)
No	3	5	30	51	9	98 (65.3)
Total	7 (4.7)	5 (3.3)	51 (34.0)	75 (50.0)	12 (8.0)	150 (100.0)

Note: Figures in parentheses are row percentage.

The responses shows that 34.7 per cent receive some help from the bank or in nursing their accounts. In a relative sense those who were investing in fixed capital in the range of Rs. 15-25 lakh are getting such advice. Beside this group, the units that are investing in the range of Rs. 25-50 lakh or above Rs. 50 lakh also displays such a tendency; but in the case of those who invested less than Rs. 5 lakh in fixed capital, those who receive the advice are more in a number than those who did not get such an advice. Contrary to this in a case of Rs. 5-15 lakhs group a majority are not getting any advice in nursing their accounts like those in a higher ranges of capital investment.

Usually it is expected that business people may get the advice better than other groups in nursing their accounts, but in a relative sense it is those who are having an agricultural back ground that received mostly the advice on nursing their accounts.

Table 5.14

Caste-wise Differences in Nursing Accounts and Assistance from Financial Institutions

Nursing the accounts by financial institutions	*Other Castes*	*Backward Class*	*Scheduled Castes*	*Scheduled Tribes*	*Total*
Yes	42	8	1	1	52 (34.7)
No	77	14	5	2	98 (65.3)
Total	119 (79.3)	22 (14.7)	6 (4.0)	3 (2.0)	150 (100.0)

Note: Figures in parentheses are row percentage.

To the question regarding nursing the accounts or advice from institutions in each caste those who said 'No' outnumber those who said 'Yes'. Among those who said 'Yes' the relative percentage is higher for backward classes than other castes.

In the case of respondents educated up to SSC, Degree and post graduation, the relative percentage is higher for those who said 'No' than those who said 'Yes'. But in the case of those who studied XII standard the number of those who said 'Yes' is higher than those who said 'No'. Thus even those who have higher educational qualifications could not receive much help from the institutions.

Table 5.15
Assistance from Financial Institutions as per the Educational Qualifications of the Respondents

Nursing the accounts by financial institutions	*SSC*	*XII Std*	*Degree*	*Post - Graduate*	*Total*
Yes	6	14	24	8	52 (34.7)
No	15	13	47	23	98 (65.3)
Total	21 (4.0)	27 (18.0)	71 (47.3)	31 (20.7)	150 (100.0)

Note: Figures in parentheses are row percentage.

Another question had been put whether they approached higher officials in the bank/public financial institutions for meeting their financial needs 87.3 per cent have said they approached the higher officials in the bank and other financial institutions. The castewise figures show that in the case of OC's and BC's the gap between those who said 'Yes' and those who said 'No' is relatively high. But all the SC's and ST's had approached the bankers for financial assistance.

Table 5.16
Caste-wise Responses for Getting Financial Assistance

Required to approach higher officials in the banks	*Other Castes*	*Backward Class*	*Scheduled Castes*	*Scheduled Tribes*	*Total*
Yes	101	21	6	3	131 (87.3)
No	18	1	-	-	19 (12.7)
Total	119 (79.3)	22 (14.7)	6 (4.0)	3 (2.0)	150 (100.0)

Note: Figures in parentheses are row percentage.

Table 5.17
Financial Assistance as per Educational Qualifications

Required to approach higher officials in the banks	*SSC*	*XII Std*	*Degree*	*Post -Graduate*	*Total*
Yes	20	25	59	27	131 (87.3)
No	1	2	12	4	19 (12.7)
Total	21 (4.0)	27 (18.0)	71 (47.3)	31 (20.7)	150 (100.0)

Note: Figures in parentheses are row percentage.

Even considering the educational qualification a majority under each educational qualification has to approach higher officials in banks. Among those who has greater educational attainment, a relatively higher number did not approach the bankers.

Table 5.18
Accepting Deposits/Taking Loans from the Public

Response	*Frequency*	*Percentage*
Yes	21	14.0
NO	129	86.0
Total	150	100.0

Note: Figures in parentheses are row percentage.

A small number of units, which had invested a higher amount in fixed capital, often invite investment by public for raising their capital. This may take the form of either collection of deposits or loans from the public. When a question had been put to the respondents whether they accept deposits or take loans from the public 14 per cent replied in the affirmative, indicating that this form of raising finances is limited to only a few units in the sample.

Table 5.19
Total Value of Sales

(in lakhs of Rs.)

Sales in Lakhs of Rs.	*1993-94*		*1994-95*		*1995-96*		*1996-97*		*1997-98*	
	No.	*Percent*	*No.*	*Percent*	*No.*	*Percent*	*No.*	*Percent*	*No.*	*Percent*
0-10	57	38.0	52	34.7	35	23.3	22	14.7	6	0.7
10-20	35	23.3	30	20.0	32	21.3	32	21.3	49	32.7
20-30	37	24.7	47	31.3	50	33.3	60	40.0	40	26.7
30-40	12	8.0	12	8.0	22	14.7	20	13.3	33	22.0
40-50	5	3.3	2	1.3	3	2.0	7	4.7	10	6.7
50-75	2	1.3	4	2.7	1	0.7	4	2.7	7	4.7
Above 75	2	1.3	3	2.0	7	4.7	5	3.3	10	6.7
Total	150	100.0	150	100.0	150	100.0	150	100.0	150	100.0

Note: Figures in parentheses are row percentage.

Growth Pattern of Sales and Principal Markets of the Sample Units

Entrepreneurship is a trait that reflects the ingenuity of entrepreneur in the improvement of the sales from year to year. The data of sales on all products from all the units for the period 1993-1998 had been collected. Year-wise comparisons of sales show that the firms had experienced relatively higher sales in some year and lower sales in other years. Firms which are having sales for less than Rs. 10 lakh formed 38 per cent of the total in 1993-94. This percentage had declined from year to year and had become 34.7; 23.3; 14.7; 0.7 in 1994-95; 1995-96; 1996-97 and 1997-98 respectively. Thus expect for one firm by 1997-98 all the firms had shown improvement in the sales in subsequent years.

In the next range of Rs. 10-20 lakh the percentages over the years had shown small variations upto 1996-97, but it had shown a sudden change in 1997-98; that is from 21.3 per cent in 1996-97 it increased to 32.7 per cent in 1997-98. In the next range of Rs. 20-30 lakhs there had been a steady improvement in the percentage up to 1996-97; that is from 24.7 per cent in 1993-94; it had increased to 31.3 per cent in 1994-95, later it increased to 33.3 per cent in 1995-96 and 40.0 per cent in 1996-97 but in 1997-98 it had declined to 26.7 per cent.

In the next range of Rs. 30-40 lakh there had been no change in the first two years, the percentage remained at 8. But in 1995-96 it improved to 14.7 per cent and showed a slight variation and had become 13.3 per cent in 1996-97 but it once again has shown improvement and became 22 per cent in 1997-98. In the higher ranges of sales there had been variations from year to year. From 1995-96 onwards there had been steady increase in the percentage among those firms that reported sales between Rs. 40-50 lakh and Rs. 50-75 lakh. Thus the percentage is observed to be 2.0 in 1995-96 in the range of Rs. 40-50 lakh but it became 6.7 per cent by the year 1997-98. Likewise in the next range it became 4.7 per cent in 1997-98. In the next interval of Rs. 50-75 lakh, the percentage increased from 0.7 in 1995-96 to

4.7 in 1997-98. For the total sales of all products valued about Rs. 75 lakh from 1993-94 there had been a steady rise in the percentage; but in 1996-97 it became 3.3 and it became 6.7 in 1997-98.

Thus in 1997-98 the sales position had undergone certain changes where there had been an improvement in the number of firms having their sales either for less than Rs. 20 lakhs or for more than Rs. 30 lakh. The firms which are having sales for less than Rs. 10 lakh had declined in number over the years even though there have been certain small variations here also. The overall improvement in the sales of a major number of firms is an indicator that entrepreneurship of those firms had been dynamic enough to adopt themselves to the changing market conditions.

In order to ascertain how the firms could bring about an improvement in sales an analysis had been done to consider the relative sales of the firms between 1993-94 and 1997-98.

In 1993-94 there were 57 units which were having sales for less than Rs. 10 lakh but by 1997-98 a considerable number of units had shown improvement in sales. For instance 49 units had been having sales in the range of Rs. 10-20 lakh in 1997-98 which became possible as many firms had improved their performance, but there are other units which had shown remarkable progress by 1997-98 in their sales. There were 3 units that had improved their position to 40-50 lakh range, 3 units to 50-75 lakh range and 5 units to above 75 lakh even with in one year, that is from 1996-97 to 1997-98. Thus in all the above case it is evident that entrepreneurship is playing major role. Thus the analysis indicates that a majority of the firms have either maintained their earlier position or had shown an improvement in their sales, which signifies that entrepreneurs of these units are dynamic in adopting themselves to the new market conditions and over a five years period they could improve their position.

Usually the firms sell their products on cash terms. But in the case of small scale units, since some of them are ancillary units to large-scale firms, sales may be done on credit terms also. When a question had been put to the units whether they sell their product on cash terms, 67.3 per cent of the firms replied that they sell on credit terms while others said that they sell on cash terms primarily, as each firm may be having part of the sales on credit terms and remaining on cash terms. To another question about the duration of the period for which credit will be allowed, 40.7 per cent of the firms said that it is below 30 days, 31.3 per cent said that it will be below 120 days and in the case of only one firm the duration is for less than 180 days. Thus a significant number of firms allow only 30 days duration.

Table 5.20
Terms of Sales

Terms of Sales	*Less than 30 days*	*Less than 120 days*	*Less than 180 days*	*Total*
Credit basis	61 (40.7)	47 (31.3)	1 (0.7)	109 (72.7)
Cash basis	41 (27.3)	-	-	41 (27.3)
TOTAL	102 (68.0)	47 (31.3)	1 (0.7)	150 (100.0)

Note: Figures in parentheses are row percentage and column percentage.

Table 5.21
Price Fixation for the Products

Nature of the price fixed	*Frequency*	*Percentage*
Wholesale	120	80.0
Retail	29	19.3
Did not specify	1	0.7
Total	150	100.0

Note: Figures in parentheses are row percentage.

When a question had been asked about what type of price prevails for their products, that is whole sale or retail, 80 per cent said that for their products they charge wholesale price. In the case of 19.3 per cent of the firms it is retail prices and only one unit did not specify the type of price charged for their products.

Table 5.22
Nature of Discount Allowed for the Products

Nature of the price fixed	*Frequency*	*Percentage*
Cash	136	90.7
Quantity	14	9.3
Total	150	100.0

Note: Figures in parentheses are row percentage.

To another question about the nature of discount allowed, 90.7 per cent of the firms said that they allow cash discount while in the case of 9.3 per cent of the firms quantity discounts are allowed. Thus cash discount in the prevalent form for allowing discount by the entrepreneurs.

Table 5.23
Channels of Distribution for the Products

Channel of Distribution	*Frequency*	*Percentage*
Direct to the ultimate consumer	36	24.0
Through the retailer	47	31.3
Specialized wholesaler	41	27.3
Agent/Broker (Distributors)	26	17.3
Total	150	100.0

Note: Figures in parentheses are row percentage.

For every firm, the channel of distributions of the product has a place of importance, as it will be a determining factor for the growth of sales. Hence a question had been asked how they are marketing their products; 24 per cent said that they sell their products directly to the consumers; supplying through the retailer is the channel adopted by 31.3 per cent of the firms for marketing their products. In the case of 27.3 per cent of the sample units the channel utilized by the firms had been specialized wholesalers. Agencies or Distributors supplied the products for 17.3 per cent of the firms. Thus a majority of the firms that is about 3/4th of the sample units utilized other channles to sell their products. Here also one fourth of the total sample units directly deal with consumers. Hence other channels of distribution had a prominent role in the marketing process of the product produced by the small-scale units.

Table 5.24

Sales Organisation in the Unit

Response	*Frequency*	*Percentage*
Wholesale	85	56.7
Retail	64	42.7
Did not specify	1	0.7
Total	150	100.0

Note: Figures in parentheses are row percentage.

To another question whether the firms have a sales organization in their unit, 56.7 per cent of the units had replied in the affirmative. Here also except for one unit the remaining units, that is 42.7 per cent have said No. Thus a considerable percentage of the units have their sales organization reflecting that the small scale units are also following the mode of operation of the large scale units for selling their products.

One of the trends of entrepreneurship is locating the demand for the product which can be within the country or outside the country. In the case of some forms the nature of the

Table 5.25

Responses regarding Principal Markets of the Firms in 1995-96,1996-97 & 1997-98

Percentage share in the market	*Local*			*Within the State*			*Within the Country*			*Experts*		
	1995-96	*1996-67*	*1997-98*	*1995-96*	*1996-67*	*1997-98*	*1995-96*	*1996-67*	*1997-98*	*1995-96*	*1996-67*	*1997-98*
Less than 25	40 (26.7)	34 (22.7)	11 (7.3)	146 (97.3)	148 (98.7)	147 (98.0)	82 (54.7)	74 (49.3)	54 (36.0)	134 (89.3)	130 (86.7)	130 (86.7)
25-50	39 (26.0)	28 (18.7)	26 (17.3)	3 (2.0)	1 (0.7)	1 (0.7)	16 (10.7)	19 (12.7)	29 (19.3)	10 (6.7)	11 (7.5)	13 (8.7)
50-75	51 (34.0)	63 (42.0)	68 (45.3)	1 (0.7)	1 (0.7)	2 (1.3)	33 (22.0)	35 (23.3)	35 (23.3)	4 (2.7)	9 (6.0)	5 (3.3)
Above 75	20 (43.3)	25 (16.7)	45 (30.0)	-	-	-	19 (12.7)	22 (14.7)	32 (21.3)	2 (1.3)	-	2 (1.3)
Total	150 (100.0)	150 (100.0)	150 (100.0)	150 (100.0)	150 (100.0)	150 (100.0)	150 (100.0)	150 (100.0)	150 (100.0)	150 (100.0)	150 (100.0)	150 (100.0)

Note: Figures in parenthesis are row percentage and column percentage.

product may be such that product may be having demand in the local markets only. There could be some products for which the demand for their products may be in the markets distributed within the state or within the country. Hence the role of entrepreneurs is paramount in such cases where the entrepreneur takes advantage of the demand for the product beyond local markets. Hence a question had been asked as to what extent the product has been sold in a different market. Data had been collected for three years namely 1995-96; 1996-97 and 1997-98.

In the case of the product being sold in the local market, the percentage in different years show certain variations. For instance in 1996-97, 26.7 per cent of the firms were selling less than 25 per cent of their products in the local markets. But by 1997-98 this percentage had become 7.3 per cent; likewise 26 per cent of the firms were selling less than 50 per cent in local markets and this percentage had become 17.3 per cent in 1997-98. But in the case of the firms selling less than 75 per cent of the total production, the percentage of the firms increased from 34 in 1995-96 to 42 in 1996-97 and to 45.3 in 1997-98. Likewise the proportion of firms which are selling in between 75 and 100 per cent had also increased steadily from 13.3 in 1995-96 to 16.7 per cent in 1996-97 and to 30.0 in 1997-98. In 1997-98 there are two firms which are selling their total production in the local market only. Thus a large number of firms are increasing their sales in the local markets in the period under consideration.

In the case of firms selling within the state 97.3 per cent were selling less than 25 per cent of the total production within the state in 1995-96 and this percentage had changed to 98.7 in 1996-97 and to 98 per cent in 1997-98. In 1995-96 there were three firms selling in between 25-50 percentage within the state. But by 1997-98 only one firm is selling in this range but in the next range there was one firm in 1995-96 and it became two firms in 1997-98. Thus a majority of the firms are selling a very low percentage of their total output within the state, which indicates that they are selling in other markets relatively at a higher percentage. Thus we find some of the firms selling in relatively higher percentages within the country. In 1995-96, 54.7 per cent are selling less than 25 per cent of the total output within the country, but this percentage had declined to 36 in 1997-98. On the other hand there had been improvement in the case of all the other firms in other higher ranges. Especially there was one firm which was selling all its total output within the country in 1996-97. By 1997-98 this number had become 5 indicating that there are more firms now selling their total out put within the country.

A small number of firms are attempting to export their products to other countries. In 1995-96, 89.3 per cent of the firms are selling less then 25 per cent of their products in other countries. This percentage had declined to 86.7 per cent indicating that some firms have improved their export performance. In 1995-96, 6.7 firms were exporting in the range of 25-50 per cent, but this had become 7.3 in 1996-97 and 8.7 in 1997-98. Likewise 2.7 per cent of firms were exporting in the range of 50-75 per cent. In 1995-96 and it became 3.3 per cent in 1997-98. In the case of firms exporting more than 75 per cent of the total output. The number remained the same in 1995-96 and 1997-98 although their performance declined in the year 1996-97. Thus we find that there were 20 firms which are engaged in export trade where their exports were for more than 25 per cent of their total output in 1996-97 as well as in 1997-98. This analysis shows that a majority of firms are either selling their products locally or with in the county.

Table 5.26
Competition from Large Scale Units

Response	*Frequency*	*Percentage*
YES	74	59.3
NO	76	50.7
Total	150	100.0

Source: Field Survey.

Table 5.26(A)
Form of the Competition

Form	*Frequency*	*Percentage*
Not facing competition	53	35.3
Price	14	9.3
Quality	26	17.3
Marketing practice	55	36.7
Others	2	1.3
Total	150	100.0

Source: Field Survey.

The industrial structure in India is such that there is often competition between large scale units and small scale units in certain lines of production. Hence the entrepreneurs of the small scale units face competition from large scale units. When a question had been put whether they were facing any competition from large scale units, 49.3 per cent of firms said 'Yes' while the remaining 50.7 per cent replied 'No'. When a probe was made about the form of the competition, 35.3 per cent of the respondents were of the opinion that there was no competition from large scale firms. Among those who replied that competition from large scale units exists, 9.3 per cent attributed it to price differences; 17.3 per cent attributed it to quality; 36.7 per cent were of the opinion that marketing practices differ while other reasons such as window display had been mentioned by only 2 units. Thus differences in marketing practices has been found to be a major factor in the competition between small scale and large scale units.

The small scale units require export promotion schemes as they enhance their exports to other countries. Hence a question had been put whether they have export promotions schemes and if the schemes are there how they could improve the performance vis-à-vis another country. In the total sample 8 per cent said they do not have any idea while 68.7 per cent said that they were not benefited by any such scheme, only

23.3 per cent of the firms said that there were export promotions schemes.

Table 5.27
Utilisation of Expert Promotion Schemes

Response	*Frequency*	*Percentage*
Yes	35	23.3
No	103	68.7
Did'nt specify	12	8.0
Total	150	100.0

Source: Field Survey.

Profits of the Sample Units

Entrepreneurs' ability is reflected in how best they can make profits in higher ranges in a sustained manner. Most of the firms are organized either on sole trade basis or on partnership basis. Entrepreneurs have more freedom to take decisions unlike in the joint stock company where board of directors have a major say in decision making. Hence the profit making by the entrepreneurs is influenced only by certain social indicators like caste or may also be influenced by the capital invested in the firm. Hence an analysis had been made here to ascertain the relationships of profits with the above indicators.

In 1995-96 there were 27 firms making profits of less than Rs. 5,000, of these a relatively higher percentage of the firms are from those firms having fixed capital in the interval of Rs. 15-25 lakh; it is pertinent to note here that there were two firms each in the Rs. 26-50 lakh category and above Rs. 50 lakh category. By 1996-97 the firms earned less than Rs. 5,000 profits have come down to 18 and in this year also 9 firms having fixed capital in the interval of Rs. 16-25 lakh and above Rs. 50 lakh range can be found. But by 1997-98 there are only 4 firms in less than Rs. 5,000 category and there is one firm in the above Rs. 50 lakh category.

Table 5.28

Profits Earned by the Firms as per their Fixed Capital Investment

Profits	*Investment in Fixed Capital (in Lakhs of Rs.)*								
	Below 5			*5-10*			*15-25*		
(in thousands)	*1995-96*	*1996-97*	*1997-98*	*1995-96*	*1996-67*	*1997-98*	*1995-96*	*1996-67*	*1997-98*
Less than 5	2	2	-	7	5	1	14	9	2
5-10	2	2	3.0	8	11	12	8	11	19
10-15	11	9	6	14	15	13	23	23	17
15-20	-	2	5	7	4	5	7	9	12
20-25	-	-	1	-	1	4	-	-	2
above 25	-	-	-	2	2	3	1	1	1
Total	15 (10.0)	15 (10.0)	15 (10.0)	38 (25.3)	38 (25.3)	38 (25.3)	53 (35.3)	53 (35.3)	53 (35.3)

Profits	*25-50*			*Above 50*			*Total*		
(in thousands)	*1995-96*	*1996-97*	*1997-98*	*1995-96*	*1996-67*	*1997-98*	*1995-96*	*1996-67*	*1997-98*
Less than 5	2	1	-	2	1	1	27	18	4
5-10	9	7	8	6	3	4	33	34	46
10-15	13	13	9	4	7	2	65	67	47
15-20	4	5	6	1	2	3	19	22	31
20-25	2	2	4	1	1	2	3	4	13
Above 25	-	2	3	-	-	2	3	5	9
Total	30 (20.0)	30 (20.0)	30 (20.0)	14 (9.3)	14 (9.3)	14 (9.3)	150 (100.0)	150 (100.0)	150 (100.0)

Note: Figures in parentheses are row percentage.

In the next range of Rs. 5-10 thousand there is not much change in the number of firms earning profits in this interval between 1995-96 and 1996-97 as the total increased from 33 to 34. The firms are distributed in all the ranges of fixed capital investment, though the number is same in the higher ranges. In 1995-96 the number is more in the lower ranges that is Rs. 5-15 lakh and Rs. 15-25 lakh in 1996-97. But in 1997-98 the number of firms increased substantially from 34 to 46 and in the above lower ranges, we find a considerable number of firms making their profits.

In Rs.10-15 thousand class interval we find 14 units in 1995-96; the number increased to 15 in 1996-97 but declined to 13 in 1997-98. In all the years the number of firms having lesser capital investment could improve their position, especially in the below Rs. 5 lakh category but the firms which were in the ranges of 15-25 lakh and 25-50 lakh have remained the same in 1996-97 as 1995-96, but in 1997-98 we find the firms relative position changing in all the higher ranges of fixed capital investment, the number of firms declined.

In Rs. 15-20 thousand category we find the number of firms making profits in this range steadily increased from year to year. By 1997-98 we find improvement in the number of firms in all categories of investment in fixed capital. Even in the case of firms having less than Rs. 5 lakh as their investment the number increased from 2 to 5.

In the higher ranges of profits that is Rs. 20-25 thousand and above Rs. 25 thousand the number of firms steadily increased over the years. Here also there is an improvement in the number of firms earning profits in Rs. 20-25 thousand range. Likewise we find two firms having above Rs. 50 lakh investment earning profits in the above 25 thousand category.

Profits may be positively related to the working capital that is invested by the firms. In the case of the firms investing below Rs. 5 lakh in working capital, 8 firms were earning profits below Rs. 5 thousnad in 1995-96. Their number became 5 in 1996-97 and nil by 1997-98. Thus there is no firm earning profits

Table 5.29
Profits Earned by the Firms as per their Investment in Working Capital

Profits (in thousands)	*Investment in Fixed Capital (in Lakhs of Rs.)*								
	Below 5			*5-10*			*15-25*		
	1995-96	*1996-97*	*1997-98*	*1995-96*	*1996-67*	*1997-98*	*1995-96*	*1996-67*	*1997-98*
Less than 5	8	5	-	13	8	3	3	2	-
5-10	3.0	4	5	13	17	22	4	6	9
10-15	3	5	7	28	27	20	4	13	9
15-20	-	-	2	10	11	14	6	6	6
20-25	-	-	-	-	1	4	-	-	3
Above 25	-	-	-	2	2	3	-	-	-
Total	14 (9.3)	14 (9.3)	14 (9.3)	66 (44.0)	66 (44.0)	66 (44.0)	27 (18.0)	27 (18.0)	27 (18.0)

(Contd...)

Profits (in thousands)	*25-50*			*Above 50*			*Total*		
	1995-96	1996-97	1997-98	1995-96	1996-67	1997-98	1995-96	1996-67	1997-98
Less than 5	3	3	-	-	-	1	27 (18.0)	18 (12.0)	4 (2.7)
5-10	8	5	6	5	2	4	33 (22.0)	34 (22.7)	46 (30.7)
10-15	9	11	5	11	11	6	65 (43.3)	67 (44.7)	47 (31.3)
15-20	2	2	5	1	3	4	19 (12.7)	22 (14.7)	31 (20.7)
20-25	3	2	5	-	1	1	3 (2.0)	4 (2.7)	13 (8.7)
Above 25	-	2	4	1	1	2	3 (2.0)	5 (3.3)	9 (6.0)
Total	25 (16.7)	25 (16.7)	25 (16.7)	18 (12.0)	18 (12.0)	18 (12.0)	150 (100.0)	150 (100.0)	150 (100.0)

Note: Figures in parentheses are row and column percentages.

for less than Rs.5 thousand in 1997-98 on the other hand there is one firm investing more than 50 lakh having profits less than Rs. 5,000 in 1997-98. In rhe case of higher ranges of working capital, the number of firms earning les than Rs. 5,000 had almost become nil by 1997-98 except for 3 firms in Rs. 6-15 lakh interval. Thus the number of firms earning profits for less than Rs. 5,000 had declined from 27 in 1995-96 to 4 in 1997-98.

In the case of firms earning profits in the range of Rs. 5-10 thousand, the number of firms increased from 33 in 1995-96 to 42 in 1997-98. This increase in the number is more pronounced in the case of firms investing in the range of Rs.5-15 lakhs but in the next higher range profits of Rs.10-15 thousands, the number had declined from 65 in 1995-96 to 47 in 1997-98. Except in the case of firms investing less than 5 lakhs, in all other ranges of investments, the number had declined in 1997-98 compared to 1995-96. The change in the position of the firms indicates that in the above Rs. 50 lakh category the number has come down from 11 in 1995-96 to 6 in 1997-98 indicating that some of the firms either moved to higher ranges of profits or to lower ranges of profits. A perusal of the table shows that 2 firms could have moved to the higher ranges of profits, while 3 firms might have earned less profits. Likewise we see shifts in the case of Rs. 5-15, 15-25 and Rs. 25-50 lakh intervals and the number had declined more in the case of Rs. 5-15 lakh group, the possibility being some firms are earning more profits in 1997-98 over 1995-96. Thus we find the number increasing in the case of different classes of working capital for Rs.15-20 thousand profit range, the exception being those firms that invested in the range of Rs. 15-25 lakh, the number remaining at 6 in all the three years. An interesting aspect is by 1997-98 there were two firms in the below 5 lakh category earning profits in 15-20 thousand class interval. In a similar manner there had been remarkable increase in a number of firms in remaining profits in the range of Rs. 20 to 25 thousand. As it increased from 3 in 1995-96 to 13 in 1997-98. The same tendency can be observed in the case of above Rs. 25 thousand group. Thus as the working capital is increasing the profits had also been increasing but

Table 5.30
Profits Earned by the Firms as per their Caste of the Respondents

Profits (in lakhs)	Caste of the Respondents														
	Other castes			Backward classes			Scheduled castes			Scheduled tribes			Total		
	1995-96	1996-97	1997-98	1995-96	1996-97	1997-98	1995-96	1996-97	1997-98	1995-96	1996-97	1997-98	1995-96	1996-97	1997-98
Less than 5	21	14	3	4	2	1	2	2	-	-	-	-	27 (18.0)	18 (12.0)	4 (2.7)
5-10	27	29	37	4	4	7	1	1	2	1	-	-	33 (22.0)	34 (22.7)	46 (30.7)
10-15	49	50	37	11	13	7	3	2	3	2	2	2	65 (43.3)	67 (44.7)	47 (20.7)
15-20	17	20	25	2	1	4	-	1	-	-	-	2	19 (12.7)	22 (14.7)	31 (20.7)
20-25	2	1	10	1	2	2	-	-	1	-	1		3 (2.0)	4 (3.7)	3 (8.7)
Above 25	3	5	7	-	-	1	-	-	-	-	-	1	3 (2.0)	5 (3.3)	9 (6.0)
Total	119 (79.3)	119 (79.3)	119 (79.3)	22 (14.7)	22 (14.7)	22 (14.7)	6 (4.0)	6 (4.0)	6 (4.0)	25 (16.7)	25 (16.7)	25 (16.7)	150 (100.0)	150 (100.0)	150 (100.0)

Note: Figures in parentheses are row percentage and column percentage.

this phenomena of increasing profits can be observed more so in the case of firms having working capital in the range of Rs. 5-15 lakh.

One hypothesis often assumed is that educational attainment has a positive relationship to entrepreneurial ability in making more profits. Among those who are educated up to SSC, though we find 5 firms earning profits for less than Rs. 5000 in 1995-96, by 1997-98 there is no firm in this posifion. The improvement is often seen in the case of Rs. 5-10 thousand , Rs. 15-20 thousand and above Rs. 25 thousand intervals. But there is a decline in the case of Rs. 10-15 thousand interval between 1995-96 and 1997-98. Thus we find there is an improvement in the case of firms earning profits at lower level and also in the last category that is above Rs. 25 thousand. In the case of those who are educated up to 12th class the number declined from 6 in 1995-96 to 1 in 1997-98. In the less than Rs. 5000 group, while it declined from 10 in 1995-96 to 7 in Rs. 5-10 thousand. But there a slight improvement from 8 in 1995- 96 to 7 in Rs. 5-10 thousand, from 2 to 6 in Rs. 15-20 thousands and from 1 to in Rs. 20-25 thousand. There is one firm earning above Rs. 25 thousands in the year 1997-98. Thus there is an improvement in profits earning by the firms in this group between 1995-96 and 1997-98. In the case of those who are graduates the number declared from 9 in 1995-96 to 2 in 1997-98 in the less than Rs.5000 group but it improved from 15 to 24 in Rs. 5-10 thousand. In Rs. 10-15 thousand once again the number declined from 33 in 1995-96 to 21 but it increased from 11 to 13 in Rs. 15-20 thousand and from 0 to 8 in Rs. 20-25 thousand. Thus there was much improvement in the case of the firms in this group. In the case of those who have done their post graduation the number declined from 7 in 1995-96 to 1 in 1997-98 for less than Rs. 5000 group but it improved from 2 to 8 for Rs. 5 -1 0 thousand in the case of Rs. 10- 15 it declined from 17 to 11 but it increased from 5 to 9 for Rs. 15 -20 thousands. There are 2 firms earning in the interval of Rs. 20-25 thousands in 1997-98. Thus though there are changes in the profits earned by the firms; we find more number of firms in the lower ranges than in the higher ranges.

Table 5.31
Profits Earned by the Firms as per their Educational Qualifications

Profits	Educational Qualifications														
	SSC			XII Std			Degree			Post-graduate			Total		
(in lakhs)	1995-96	1996-97	1997-98	1995-96	1996-97	1997-98	1995-96	1996-97	1997-98	1995-96	1996-97	1997-98	1995-96	1996-97	1997-98
Less than 5	5	4	-	6	4	1	9	5	2	7	5	1	27 (18.0)	18 (12.0)	4 (2.7)
5-10	6	6	7	10	6	7	15	19	24	2	3	8	33 (22.0)	34 (22.7)	46 (30.7)
10-15	7	6	5	8	11	10	33	32	21	17	18	11	65 (43.3)	67 (44.7)	47 (20.7)
15-20	1	2	3	2	4	6	11	11	13	5	5	9	19 (12.7)	22 (14.7)	31 (20.7)
20-25	2	1	1	1	2	2	-	1	8	-	-	2	3 (2.0)	4 (3.7)	3 (8.7)
above 25	-	2	5	-	-	1	3	3	3	-	-	2	3 (2.0)	5 (3.3)	9 (6.0)
Total	21 (14.0)	21 (14.0)	21 (14.0)	27 (18.0)	27 (18.0)	27 (18.0)	71 (47.3)	71 (47.3)	71 (47.3)	31 (20.7)	31 (20.7)	31 (20.7)	150 (100.0)	150 (100.0)	150 (100.0)

Note: Figures in parentheses are row percentage and column percentage.

Thus this analysis shows that higher education attainment may not be such a decisive factor in earning more profits.

Table 5.32
Continuance in the Same Line of Production

Response	*Frequency*	*Percentage*
Yes	12	68.0
No	48	32.0
Total	150	100.0

Note: Figures in parentheses are row percentage.

As most firms had been earning profits in 1997-98, the firms which were incurring losses were not reported in the sample even though some firms were earning profits in the less Rs. 5000 interval they were erning same amount, may be very small in some cases. Therefore none had replied the reasons for making losses; hence no body could tell what were their plans to reduce the losses. When they were asked a question to narrate their experiences, the entrepreneurs have given information about their years of experience as an entrepreneur. All the entrepreneurs in the sample are having a mimmum experience of 3 years. To a question whether they would like to continue in the same industry or line of manufacture, 68 per cent said 'Yes' and 32 per cent said 'No'. Hence many would like to continue in the same line of manufacture.

In the next chapter, some findings pertaining to entrepreneurship and promotion of small scale industry will be presented.

The above analysis brings out that a majority of entrepreneurs had replaced their machinery and even others are also planning to replace their machinery in the next two years. Institutional finance, instead of utilisation of interval surplus, is playing an important role for the expansion of their capacity in the last five years. Caste-wise differences are not significant in expanding the capacity of the firm. Very low profit earners and very high profit earners are able to take the decision to expand their firms in the next two years.

Firms could improve their sales over the last five years, which is indicative of a dynamic entrepreneurship. Which selling in the local markets had increased in the last three years, firms are also improving their sales in the national markets as well as international markets. While half of the sample units face competition from large scale units, it is mainly attributed to the market practices pursued by the large scale units. For all categories firm having variations in the capital structure in object of fixed capital, the number of firms earning profits from their working capital structure, firms having working capital in the middle range could improve their profits to a considerable extent. Other castes could improve their position as they moved from a lower range of profits to a higher range of profits over time in comparison with other castes, though they could also improve their profits earning capacity. It was also found that higher educational attainment need not be a decisive factor for earning profits. A majority expressed the opinion that they would like to continue in the same line of production in the coming years reflecting their confidence in managing their affairs.

6

Entrepreneurship and Promotion of Small Scale Industry: Some Findings

Entrepreneurship requires some fostering as a firm has to be nurtured since its inception. For this purpose different institutions are playing a role in the early stages as well as at later stages.

Financing of the Enterprises

The Table 6.1 indicates how some of the institutions are participating in the growth of different production units.

Among the various institutions that played a key role at the time of the starting of the units, banks and DIC have a major role, though other institutions like SFC, ICICI, IDBI have also extended financial help for setting up of the units. Almost 1/3rd of the units received financial assistance from banks. Banks assistance had been of a higher proportion in Warangal, Karimnagar, Khammam and Adilabad. In the case of DIC the relative percentage is higher for Adilabad when compared to other districts. In the case of other institutions Karimnagar had a higher percentage than the other three districts. Thus the DICs, which are expected to play a major role in the setting up of the units, had a better role in Adilabad districts than the other three districts and a fact that emerged from this sample study is that other agencies have rendered financial assistance for starting the units to a more number of units than banks or DIC.

Table 6.1
Institutions for Promoting the Industrial Units

(in Percentages)

S. No.	*Name of the Institutions*	*Frequency with Percentage*				*Total Frequency with percentage*
		Adilabad	*Karimnagar*	*Khammam*	*Warangal*	
1.	Banks	02(16.67) (3.7)	07(35) (13.0)	25(33.34) (46.3)	20(46.51) (37.01)	54(36) (100.0)
2.	DIC	08(66.67) (20.5)	03(15) (7.7)	18(24.00) (46.2)	10(23.26) (25.6)	39(26) (100.0)
3.	Any other (SFC, ICIC, IDBI, etc.)	02(16.67) (3.5)	10(50) (17.51)	32(42.67) (56.1)	13(30.23) (22.9)	57(38) (100.0)
	Total	12 (100.00) (8.0)	20(100.00) (13.3)	75(100.00) (50.0)	43(100.00) (28.7)	150(100.00) (100.00)

Note: Figures in parentheses are row percentages and columns percentages.

After the units started functioning entrepreneurs have mentioned supply of eletricity as well as working capital requirements have a significant role in the functioning of the units.

The institutions that are rendering assistance for the functioning of the units is mainly the uninterrupted supply of the electricity as well as meeting their working capital requirements. Among the units that are getting assistance, a majority are getting it from financial institutions. Here their relative percentages show that Warangal has a higher percentage than Adilabad or Karimnagar. In the case of electricity Khammam units are higher percentage than the other three districts. Above 20 percent of the units in Adilabad, Karimnagar and Khammam are receiving financial assistance from other institutions like SFC, ICICI, IDBI, and other institutions. Thus getting supply of electricity has also some significance ofter the units are set up.

Table 6.2
Institutional Assistance in the Second Phase

(in Percentage)

S. No.	Name of the Institutions	Frequency with Percentage Adilabad	Karimnagar	Khammam	Warangal	Total Frequency with percentage
1.	Electricity	03(25.00) (6.8)	06(30.00) (13.6)	25(33.34) (56.8)	10(23.25) (22.7)	44(29.34) (100.0)
2.	Financial Institution	06(50.00) (7.6)	10(50.00) (12.7)	35(46.67) (44.3)	28(65.1) (35.4)	79(52.17) (100.0)
3.	Any other (SFC, ICICI, IDBI, etc)	03(25.00) (11.1)	04(20.00) (14.8)	15(20.00) (55.6)	05(11.63) (18.5)	27(18.00) (100.0)
	Total	12(100.00) (8.0)	20(100.00) (13.3)	75(100.00) (50.0)	43(100.00) (28.7)	150(100.00) (100.00)

Note: Figures in parentheses are row percentages and columns percentages.

Table 6.3
Functions Performed by the Institutions

(in Percentage)

S. No.	Function Performed	Frequency with Percentage Adilabad	Karimnagar	Khammam	Warangal	Total Frequency with percent
1.	Provision of Sheds	04(33.34) (8.3)	06(30.00) (12.5)	30(40.00) (62.5)	08(18.60) (16.7)	48(32.00) (100.0)
2.	Purchasing Machinery	06(50.00) (9.5)	10(50.00) (15.9)	35(46.67) (55.6)	12(27.90) (19.0)	63(42.00) (100.0)
3.	Fixed Capital	02(16.67) (5.1)	04(20.00) (10.3)	10(13.34) (25.6)	23(53.49) (59.0)	39(26.00) (100.0)
	Total	12(100.00) (8.0)	20(100.00) (13.3)	75(100.00) (50.0)	43(100.00) (28.7)	150(100.00) (100.00)

Note: Figures in parentheses are row percentages and columns percentages.

Institutions like DIC, and in certain other cases banks and financial institutions are assisting the entrepreneurs of the 150 units for different activities in the case of 48 units, sheds have been provided. The relative percentages show that Khammam had a higher percentage than the other three districts. In the case of purchase of machinery both Adilabad and Karimnagar have equal percentage and Khammam comes next to these districts. In the case of provision of fixed capital Warangal has a higher percentage than the other three districts.

Table 6.4
Institutions' Approach to Small Industry Development

(in Percentage)

S. No.	Name of the Emphasize	Frequency with Percentage				Total Frequency with percentage
		Adilabad	Karimnagar	Khammam	Warangal	
1.	Wholly	09(75.00) (11.7)	10(50.00) (13.00)	35(46.67) (45.41)	23(53.49) (29.9)	77(51.34) (100.0)
2.	Partially	02(16.67) (4.9)	06(30.00) (14.6)	25(33.34) (61.0)	08(18.60) (19.5)	41(27.34) (100.0)
3.	Occassionally	01(8.34) (3.1)	04(20.00) (12.5)	15(20.00) (46.9)	12(27.90) (37.5)	32(21.33) (100.0)
	Total	12(100.00) (8.0)	20(100.00) (13.3)	75(100.00) (50.0)	43(100.00) (28.7)	150(100.00) (100.00)

Note: Figures in parentheses are row percentages and columns percentages.

Among the various institutions that concentrate on Small Industry development, entrepreneurs receive assistance rather wholly or partially. Among the units in the sample 50 per cent received financial assistance wholly from those institutions that emphasises small industry development, of the four districts, Adilabad has a higher percentage than the other three districts. Likewise institutions laying emphasis partially for small industrial development figure more in Khammam district than the other three districts.

Institutions that lay emphasis for small industry development occasionally figure more in Warangal than in the other three districts.

Table 6.5
Opinion About the Personnel Engaged in Training

(in Percentage)

S. No.	Motivation	Frequency with Percentage				Total Frequency with percentage
		Adilabad	Karimnagar	Khammam	Warangal	
1.	Yes	10(83.33) (8.4)	16(80.00) (13.4)	60(80.00) (50.4)	33(76.74) (27.7)	119(29.33) (100.0)
2.	No	02(16.67) (6.5)	04(20.00) (12.9)	15(20.00) (48.4)	10(23.25) (32.2)	31(20.67) (100.0)
	Total	12(100.00) (8.0)	20(100.00) (13.3)	75(100.00) (50.0)	43(100.00) (28.7)	150(100.00) (100.00)

Note: Figures in parentheses are row percentages and columns percentages.

When the respondents were asked to reveal their opinion about the trainers' capacity to motivate the entrepreneur a majority have replied in the affirmative. The districtwise responses show that a higher percentage can be found in the Adilabad district followed by Karimnagar and Khammam, in a way signifying that the motivation programme had a positive effect in a less developed district like Adilabad. Among those who replied in the negative, the relative percentage is higher in Khammam district.

Table 6.6
Opinion About the Inter-Agency Cooperation of the Institutions *(in Percentages)*

S. No.	Cooperation	Frequency with Percentage				Total Frequency with percentage
		Adilabad	Karimnagar	Khammam	Warangal	
1.	Yes	02(16.67) (2.4)	10(50.00) (11.9)	42(56.00) (50.0)	30(69.77) (35.7)	84(56.00) (100.0)
2.	No	10(83.33) (15.2)	10(50.00) (15.1)	33(44.00) (50.00)	13(30.23) (19.7)	66(44.00) (100.0)
	Total	12(100.00) (8.0)	20(100.00) (13.3)	75(100.00) (50.0)	43(100.00) (28.7)	150(100.00) (100.00)

Note: Figures in parentheses are row percentages and columns percentages.

A majority of the entrepreneurs opined that there is interagency cooperation among various institutions that rendered assistance to the units. The districtwise comparison shows that the relative percentage is higher in Warangal for this response, while it is the lowest in Adilabad. Thus in Adilabad though there is higher level of motivation among entrepreneur, due to lack of interagency cooperation there is a tardy development of the industries in the district.

Table 6.7

Sincerity of the Institution in Promoting Entrepreneurship

(in Percentage)

Category	*Cases*	*Expected observed*	*Residual*
Yes	129.00(86.00)	75.00(50.00)	54.00
No	21.00(14.00)	75.00(50.00)	-54.00
Total	150(100.00)	150(100.00)	0
Chi-Square Value	77.7600	DF...1	Significance 0000

Note: Figures in parentheses are row percentages and columns percentages.

When question has been put to the entrepreneur whether the institutions are promoting entrepreneurship with sincerity, a majority have replied in the affirmative; even Chi-Square value is significant here.

Table 6.8

Encouragement Given to the Entrepreneurs *(in Percentage)*

S. No.	*Opinion*	*Frequency with Percentage*				*Total Frequency with percentage*
		Adilabad	*Karimnagar*	*Khammam*	*Warangal*	
1.	Yes	10(83.33) (7.2)	18(90.00) (13.1)	70(93.33) (50.7)	40(93.02) (30.0)	138(92) (100.0)
2.	No	02(16.67) (16.7)	02(10.00) (16.7)	05(6.66) (41.6)	03(6.97) (25.0)	12(8.00) (100.0)
	Total	12(100.00) (8.0)	20(100.00) (13.3)	75(100.00) (50.0)	43(100.00) (28.7)	150(100.00) (100.00)

Note: Figures in parentheses are row percentages and columns percentages.

To a question whether they were attracted to set up small units due to the encouragement given to them, a majority have said 'Yes'. Among those who said 'No' the relative percentage is higher in Adilabad.

Table 6.9

Identification of Potential Entrepreneur *(in Percentage)*

S. No.	*Opinion*	*Frequency with Percentage*				*Total Frequency with percentage*
		Adilabad	*Karimnagar*	*Khammam*	*Warangal*	
1.	Govt. Policies	01(8.33) (7.7)	04(20.00) (30.8)	05(6.67) (38.5)	03(6.97) (23.0)	13(8.67) (100.0)
2.	Training	02(16.67) (7.2)	06(30.00) (21.4	10(13.33) (35.7)	10(23.25) (35.7)	28(18.67) (100.0)
3.	Cooperation of Financial Intitutions	06(50.00) (7.9)	08(40.00) (10.5)	40(53.33) (52.6)	22(51.61) (28.91)	76(50.67) (100.0)
4.	All the Above	03(25.00) (9.1)	02(10.00) (6.1)	20(26.67) (60.6)	08(18.60) (24.2)	33(22.00) (100.0)
	Total	12(100.00) (8.0)	20(100.00) (13.3)	75(100.00) (50.0)	43(100.00) (28.7)	150(100.00) (100.00)

Note: Figures in parentheses are row percentages and columns percentages.

Regarding the opinion about the procedure for identifying potential entrepreneur, the respondents have said either government policies, training or cooperation of the financial institutions or all above the methods are responsible for identification of entrepreneur. Among the responses cooperation of financial institutions had been given a higher ranking followed by a combination of all the three methods and next in important is training while government policies have been given a lower ranking. A districtwise comparison shows Khammam and Warangal having relatively higher percentage in the case of cooperation of financial Institutions, while training had a higher percentage in Karimnagar. In the case of all methods Khammam has a higher percentage than the other districts.

Thus government policies could not lead to identification of potential entrepreneur though it is often mentioned that they have a positive role in attracting entrepreneurs.

Table 6.10
Opinion About the Help and Guidance provided to Entrepreneurs by Institutions *(in Percentage)*

S. No.	*Opinion*	*Frequency with Percentage*				*Total Frequency with percentage*
		Adilabad	*Karimnagar*	*Khammam*	*Warangal*	
1.	Helpful	10(83.33) (8.5)	15(75.00) (12.7)	60(80.00) (50.8)	33(76.74) (28.0)	118(78.67) (100.0)
2.	Not helpful	02(16.67) (6.3)	05(25.00) (15.6)	15(20.00) (46.9)	10(23.25) (31.2)	32(21.33) (100.0)
	Total	12(100.00) (8.0)	20(100.00) (13.3)	75(100.00) (50.0)	43(100.00) (28.7)	150(100.00) (100.00)

Note: Figures in parentheses are row percentages and column percentages.

Opinion was elicited from entrepreneur about the help and guidances provided to them by institutions. A majority expressed their opinion that they are helpful to them. The districtwise figures show that Adilabad has a higher percentage of entrepreneurs expressing this opinion, whereas the percentage for those who said not helpful is relatively higher in Warangal.

Role of Institutions in the Promotion of SSI Units

In most of the small scale industrial units getting uninterrupted supply of electricity is one of the major problems of the units. Hence the institutions that provide financial assistance also help the units in getting the supply of electricity. Hence opinions had been collected on the role of the institutions in getting electricity supply to their units. A majority have said that the institutions are helpful to them. The percentage of the units who gave such a response is relatively higher in Adilabad district. Among those who replied that the institutions are not helpful the percentage is higher in Warangal. There are 16 units who replied that this query doesnot apply to them. Thus the institutions are also nursing the industrial units by ensuring supply of electricity to them.

Table 6.11
Role Played by the Institutions in Electricity Supply to the Unit

S. No.	Opinion	Frequency with Percentage				Total Frequency with percentage
		Adilabad	Karimnagar	Khammam	Warangal	
1.	Helpful	10(83.33) (8.9)	15(75.00) (13.4)	56(74.64) (50.0)	31(72.09) (27.8)	112(74.67) (100.0)
2.	Not helpful	01(8.33) (4.5)	03(15.00) (13.6)	10(13.33) (45.5)	08(18.60) (36.4)	22(14.67) (100.0)
3.	Does not apply	01(8.33) (6.3)	02(10.00) (12.5)	09(12.00) (56.2)	04(9.30) (25.0)	16(10.67) (100.0)
	Total	12(100.00) (8.0)	20(100.00) (13.3)	75(100.00) (50.0)	43(100.00) (28.7)	150(100.00) (100.00)

Note: Figures in parentheses are row percentages and column percentages.

Table 6.12
Assistance Rendered by Institutions regarding the Marketing of the Products

S. No.	Type of Assistance	Frequency with Percentage				Total Frequency with percentage
		Adilabad	Karimnagar	Khammam	Warangal	
1.	Yes	10(83.33) (7.7)	15(75.00) (11.5)	68(90.67) (52.3)	37(86.04) (28.5)	130(86.67) (100.0)
2.	No	02(16.67) (10.0)	05(25.00) (25.0)	07(9.33) (35.0)	06(13.95) (30.0)	20(13.33) (100.0)
	Total	12(100.00) (8.0)	20(100.00) (13.3)	75(100.00) (50.0)	43(100.00) (28.7)	150(100.00) (100.00)

Note: Figures in parentheses are row percentages and column percentages.

The S.S.I units require assistance for marketing their products as many of the units are either food processing units or granite tiles units. Here also the institutions are supposed to play a role in assisting the units. When a question had been put to the respondents a majority had been replied that they are receiving assistance from the institutions. The response is almost the same in all the districts. The relative percentage for those who did not receive assistance is slightly more in Karimnagar than in other districts.

Table 6.13
Institutions Helping the Units in the Export of Units Products *(in Percentages)*

S. No.	*Opinion*	*Frequency with Percentage*				*Total Frequency with percentage*
		Adilabad	*Karimnagar*	*Khammam*	*Warangal*	
1.	Yes	10(83.33) (7.9)	17(85.00) (13.4)	69(92.00) (54.3)	31(72.09) (24.4)	127(84.67) (100.0)
2.	No	02(16.67) (8.7)	03(15.00) (13.0)	06(8.00) (26.1)	12(27.09) (53.2)	23(15.33) (100.0)
	Total	12(100.00) (8.0)	20(100.00) (13.3)	75(100.00) (50.0)	43(100.00) (28.7)	150(100.00) (100.00)

Note: Figures in parentheses are row percentages and column percentages.

In the entrepreneurship development programme the financial and non-financial institutions are expected to provide all round assistance to the units before the units attain a reasonable rate of profit. One way by which the units can earn profit is through exports and for this they require assistance from various institutions. When a question has been put to the entrepreneurs, a majority have said 'yes' implying that the institutions are rendering help to export their products except for a relatively lower percentage in Warangal; the percentage of those who said yes is relatively higher in all three districts. Thus many of the units are able to take advantage of the help rendered by the institutions in exporting their products.

Table 6.14
Management Consultancy Service offered by the Institutions to Small Entrepreneurs

S. No.	Opinion	*Frequency with Percentage*				*Total Frequency with percentage*
		Adilabad	*Karimnagar*	*Khammam*	*Warangal*	
1.	Providing	04(33.33) (10.0)	06(30.00) (15.0)	28(37.33) (70.0)	12(27.90) (30.0)	40(26.67) (100.0)
2.	Not Providing	08(66.67) (7.3)	14(70.00) (12.7)	47(62.67) (42.7)	31(73.10) (28.2)	110(73.33) (100.0)
	Total	12(100.00) (8.0)	20(100.00) (13.3)	75(100.00) (50.0)	43(100.00) (28.7)	150(100.00) (100.00)

Note: Figures in parentheses are row percentages and column percentages.

Often the institutions also provide management consultancy services and hence a query was made about the consultancy services provided to the institutions less than one third of the total units are receiving services and the district-wise data shows that Khammam has relatively more units receiving such services than the other three districts. Thus a majority of the units responded that the institutions are not providing management consultancy services.

Table 6.15
Extension Services Offered by Institutions
(in Percentages)

S. No.	Opinion	*Frequency with Percentage*				*Total Frequency with percentage*
		Adilabad	*Karimnagar*	*Khammam*	*Warangal*	
1.	Helpful	08(66.60) (6.6)	14(70.00) (11.5)	64(85.33) (52.5)	36(83.72) (29.4)	122(81.33) (100.0)
2.	Not Helpful	04(33.33) (14.3)	06(30.00) (21.4)	11(14.67) (39.3)	07(16.27) (25.0)	28(18.67) (100.0)
	Total	12(100.00) (8.0)	20(100.00) (13.3)	75(100.00) (50.0)	43(100.00) (28.7)	150(100.00) (100.00)

Note: Figures in parentheses are row percentages and columns percentages.

Provision of extension services will go a long way in stabilising the units in their respective lines of production. As extension services are mainly provided by the institutions, the respondents were asked whether those services were helpful to them or not. A majority of the units have said that they were helpful and the relative percentage here is more in the case of Warangal and Khammam. One reason for the extension services being helpful to the entrepreneurs could be due to the active role being played by D.I.Cs in the district.

Table 6.16
Nature of Officials in Government and Institutions (in percentages)

S. No.	Opinion	Frequency with Percentage				Total Frequency with percentage
		Adilabad	Karimnagar	Khammam	Warangal	
1.	Helpful	07(58.33) (6.5)	11(55.00) (10.3)	58(77.33) (54.2)	31(72.00) (29.0)	107(71.33) (100.0)
2.	Not Helpful	05(41.67) (11.6)	09(45.00) (20.9)	17(22.67) (39.5)	12(27.90) (27.9)	43(28.67) (100.0)
	Total	12(100.00) (8.0)	20(100.00) (13.3)	75(100.00) (50.0)	43(100.00) (28.7)	150(100.00) (100.00)

Note: Figures in parentheses are row percentages and columns percentages.

Officialdom in government as well as institutions has a catalytic role in the promotion of entrepreneurship. The experiences of the entrepreneurs reveal that they are helpful for majority of the units in the sample. But district wise percentages show that the officials in Khammam and Warangal are more helpful than the officials in Adilabad and Karimnagar. Thus a relatively high percentage among the entrepreneurs in Adilabad as well as Karimnagar did not have good experiences with officials. This finding brings out the importance of officials for the growth of entrepreneurship as the number of units in both these districts are smaller when compared to the units in Khammam and Warangal.

Table 6.17
Role of Agencies and Institutions for the Development of Small Entrepreneurs

S. No.	Opinion	Frequency with Percentage				Total Frequency with percentage
		Adilabad	Karimnagar	Khammam	Warangal	
1.	Helpful	10(83.33) (8.1)	16(81.33) (13.0)	61(81.33) (49.6)	36(83.72) (29.3)	123(82.00) (100.0)
2.	Not Helpful	02(16.67) (7.4)	04(20.00) (14.8)	14(18.28) (51.19)	07(16.28) (25.9)	27(18.00) (100.0)
	Total	12(100.00) (8.0)	20(100.00) (13.3)	75(100.00) (50.0)	43(100.00) (28.7)	150(100.00) (100.00)

Note: Figures in parentheses are row percentages and column percentages.

The role of institutions for the overall development of entrepreneurship is often mentioned in the literature. Hence a probe has been made about their role being helpful for the development of small entrepreneurs. A majority of the entrepreneurs in all the districts had responded that their role was helpful. Thus the response shows that the institutions are playing a positive role for the development of entrepreneurship.

Table 6.18
Future of S.S.I./ S.S.E in the Present Socio-economic Environment

S. No.	Opinion	Frequency with Percentage				Total Frequency with percentage
		Adilabad	Karimnagar	Khammam	Warangal	
1.	Can servive at least upto 2010 year	10(83.33) (7.6)	16(80.00) (12.2)	68(90.67) (51.9)	37(86.04) (28.2)	131(87.33) (100.0)
2.	Utilized fully	02(16.67) (13.3)	03(15.00) (20.0)	05(6.67) (33.3)	05(11.62) (33.3)	15(10.00) (100.0)
3.	Any other	- -	01(5.00) (25.0)	02(2.67) (50.0)	01(2.32) (25.0)	4(2.67) (100.0)
	Total	12(100.00) (8.0)	20(100.00) (13.3)	75(100.00) (50.0)	43(100.00) (28.7)	150(100.00) (100.00)

Note: Figures in parentheses are row percentages and columns percentages.

The future of small scale industry is in jeopardy under the present business environment due to liberalisation on one hand and heavy competition from large scale industries on the other two major opinions have been expressed by the entrepreneurs. A majority in all the districts veered round to the view that they can survive for another ten years, that is at least up to the year 2010. A small minority said that their survival depends on the full utilization of their capacity. Among other susponses assistance from institutions can lend support to the units survival. Thus a majority of the units are confident that they can face the competition in future.

An analysis of the findings indicates that banks especially in Warangal and Adilabad, and District Industrial Centers(DICs) have a major role in providing financial assistance to the units. The role of the institution was considered as helpful by a majority of respondents in Adilabad. Personnel engaged in training entrepreneurs were considered as helpful, while Adilabad banks have inter agency cooperation. The financial institution, to a greater extent, are able to identify the potential entrepreneurs. A majority in Khammam expressed their opinion that institutions were providing market assistance to them. But the management consultancy services are not being provided to a majority of the firms. Such an assistance is being provided to some extent in Warangal. DICs are playing a prominent role in providing extension services. But the attitude of government officials was not considered as helpful from some of the respondents in Karimnagar and Adilabad. As regards their survival in the competitive markets, a majority expressed the opinion that they can survive in the cement line of production at least upto 2010. Thus a majority are holding a positive view about their future.

7

Summary and Conclusions

Entrepreneurship plays a significant role in the process of economic development. Joseph Schumpeter, who emphasized the importance of entrepreneurship, opined that entrepreneurs revolutionized the pattern of production by exploiting an invention, whereby they try to innovate untried technological possibilities for producing a new commodity or by opening of a new source of supply of raw materials or by organising the industry in a different manner. Therefore entrepreneurship is another form of individual leadership and hence it acquires importance in a society, especially in Societies undergoing a social transition. Economists treat entrepreneur as a distinct factor of production. Usually pure profit is considered as the marginal product of entrepreneurship. But the difficulty is that entrepreneurs cannot be treated as members of a homogenous group. Entrepreneurship, if treated as a function, may not satisfy the conditions required to define a factor of production. Hence economists were trying to analyse this functional role. For instance, Richard Cantillon observed that entrepreneurship is a matter of foresight and willingness to assume risk. This idea had been extended by Von Thunen who defined the rewards of the entrepreneur as the returns for incurring the risks which have unpredictability. This distinction between risks and uncertainty had been elaborated by another economist, Frank Knight, who surmised that the presence of uncertainty about the future may allow entrepreneurs to earn positive profits even in the case of perfect competition. Differing from this opinion Schumpeter traced all economic changes to innovation and identified innovator with the entrepreneur.

The modern view of entrepreneur emphasizes the entrepreneurial role as one of the gathering and using resources. Peter Drucker holds the view that entrepreneurship occurs when resources are redirected to progressive opportunities and this redirection of resources distinguishes the entrepreneurial role from that of the traditional management role. However, psychologists view entrepreneurs in behavioral terms as achievement oriented individuals driven to seek challenges and new accomplishments. Thus entrepreneurship in the present day business world is about the process of creating new organisations. The distinguishing factors that entrepreneurs possess are vision for growth, commitment to constructive change, persistence to gather necessary resources and energy to achieve unusual results.

Entrepreneurship is therefore considered as a trait and programmes are initiated for entrepreneurship development.

The methodology adopted in this study, including the objectives are given as here under:

1) To analyse the concept of entrepreneurship;
2) To review the empirical studies on entrepreneurship,
3) To trace the entrepreneurship development programmes and to assess the impact of these programmes on industrial sector in general and small scale industry sector in particular;
4) To explain the sociocultural profiles of entrepreneurship;
5) To make a probe into the achievements of entrepreneurs in terms of certain economic indicators; and
6) To study the behavioural aspects of entrepreneurs in promoting their business.

The hypotheses that are tested here are as follows:

1) Entrepreneurship depends on the innovative ability of the entrepreneurs.
2) The role of entrepreneurs depends on the socio-cultural factors that mould the entrepreneurs.
3) Successful entrepreneurship depends on profit making nature of the entrepreneurs.

The research design for the study is ex-post facto experimental design. In this technique the varying influence of the identical factors is usually chosen. Here in this study as more factors may be influencing entrepreneurship these factors will be analysed, especially laying stress on innovation and change. Usually two groups are chosen for such a study but here the same group before and after change is studied.

The sampling method chosen for the above research design is multistage sampling method. Initially four districts in the state of Andhra Pradesh had been chosen. These four districts are Adilabad, Karimanager, Khammam, Warangal. At the second stage in each district different production progresses have been studied and the processes that have attracted more industrial units have been considered in their study. In the next stage among these processes a sample of units had been chosen based on the investment of fixed as well as working capital that had been functioning with same success in Adilabad, Karimnagar, Khammam and Warangal.

The primary data has been collected with the help of a structured questionnaire administered to 150 respondents who are organising small scale units in the four districts. Besides administering the questionnaire, oral interviews were also conducted to collected the data. The secondary data had been collected from books, periodicals, government reports, and unpublished dissertations.

The primary data had been analysed with the help of two way and three way cross breaks. Further percentages have been calculated and statistical tools like tests of hypothesis had been conducted. A brief survey of literature on the entrepreneurship had been presented in the second chapter.

The concept of entrepreneurship had received a new dimensions with the growth of market economy. Richard Cantillon is one of the forerunners in giving a central role to the entrepreneur in the economic system. Eventhough Adam Smith, the father of economics had also discussed this concept, the role assigned to entrepreneur is that of a capitalist, among classical economists. It was J.B. Say who described entrepreneur as one who had exceptional insight into society's needs and was able to fulfil them. The concept received a new meaning when Schumpeter observed that entrepreneurship is a force in creative destruction, whereby established ways of doing things are distraught by the creation of new and better ways to get things done. Among others who defined entrepreneurs Frank Young describes entrepreneurs as a change agent. In the new business world the concept of entrepreneurship does not exclude mangers in large organisations from being entrepreneurs if they combine resources in unusual ways to create innovative new product or services.

Entrepreneurship is a composite skill, the resultant of a mix of many qualities and traits that include tangible factors like imagination and risk taking and intangible factors such as the ability to mobilise scientific and technological advances. For instance Higgins defines the term entrepreneurship as a function of seeing investment and production opportunity, organising an enterprise to undertake a new production process, raising capital, hiring labour, arranging for the supply of raw materials and getting top managers for day to day operations of the enterprise. In the present state of industrial development an individual who will set up a small industrial unit has to come from within the country and community and hence they have a much greater impact on generating the right climate for successful entrepreneurship. Entrepreneurship training in most countries of the world is being increasingly tried to promote local entrepreneurship and accelerate the base of small enterprise development.

On the basis of the degree of innovative zeal, propensity to introduce change and qualities of leadership displayed 'Danhot' classified entrepreneurs into four distinct types. They are innovating entrepreneurship which is aggressive in experimentation; imitaitve entrepreneurship which adopts successful innovations; fabian entrepreneurship that introduces changes only when loss is imminent; drone entrepreneurship that is characterised by refusal to try the new methods even at the risk of loss. Another classification distinguishes entrepreneurs into six types namely prime mover, manager, minor innovator, initiator, satellite type and local trading type. Another classification distinguishes entrepreneurs into administrative and independent types namely craft entrepreneurs, and opportunity entrepreneurs. The differences between these two categories are related to breadth of education and training, higher social awareness, involvement and ability to deal with economic and social environment and time orientation. A distinction based on the nature of industry in which an entrepreneur owns had been attempted by Hundal. The entrepreneur belonging to textile and hosiery are termed as fast progressive while those who are found in foundry and steel industries as slow progressive. Another classification is first generation entrepreneurs and second generation entrepreneurs based on their psychological characteristics. Certain theories of entrepreneurship has been propounded by thinkers like Weber, E. Hagan, Thomas Cochran, Frank Young, John, H. Kunkel and David McClelland. In the Weberian system the entrepreneurial energies are generated by religious belief like protestant ethic. According to Hagan the social group that experienced the withdrawal of status had persued vigorous entrepreneurial activity. According to Thomas Cochran an entrepreneur is a society's modal personality. Further according to Cochran the performance of an entrepreneur will be influenced by their own attitude towards their occupation, the whole expectations held by sanctioning groups and the operational requirement of the job.

Frank Young views entrepreneurship from the angle of

clusters that is ethnic communities, occupational groups or politically oriented factions. On the other hand John H. Kunkel's behavioural model is concerned with change where one need to change only certain elements of the context in which all individuals at all times are an integral part. David McClelland emphasizes the achievement aspect of the entrepreneur. The motive of n-achievement guides the actions of entrepreneurs; that is people with high n-achievements behave in an entrepreneurial way. Harbinson on the basis of an empirical study characterises all the persons who perform entrepreneurial function in a large organisation as managerial resources the functions are mentioned as managing of risk and the handling of economic uncertainty, planning and innovation. Co-ordination, administration and control and routine supervision. Peter Kilby propounded an economic model of entrepreneurship. He showed the various possible shifts in supply and demand functions pertaining to entrepreneurship. The supply function is dependent on socio-psychological variables while demand is a function of the price of all cooperating factors of production. The stock of known or transferable technology, the level of managerial organisation and consumers income. The model explains the lack of vigorous entrepreneurship in terms of various product and factor markets' imperfections, in appropriate government policies and abrupt political changes. Hence the economists suggest remedies like appropriate monetary fiscal and trade policies, removal of marketing imperfections, provisions of inputs and technical assistance to industry.

Broadly speaking the theories can be grouped under two paradigms, namely the strategic choice model and environmental determinism model. The stratagic choice model of organisational births and deaths holds that enrtepreneurial success depends primarily on the appropriateness of the individual strategies rather than on the favourableness of the environment. Hence entrepreneurship is a process of constant adaptation to and sometimes of manipulation and control of environment through strategic choice. The population -ecology model on the other hand minimises the role of entrepreneur and holds that the survival of organisation depends on the degree to which they are compatible with the environment. Hence proponents of environmental determinism have their logic and some empirical evidence to suggest that organisations are trapped into their own area and get selected out by the environment. But there are several cases of innovative entrepreneurs who have converted constraints into opportunity. For instance one of the most successful and largest textile company in India had its beginning when the textile industry was facing an unfavourable environment. Hence it had been opined that innovation is more a function of the individual strategic choices than that of environmental influences. A discrimination is made here between the general environment that consists of the economic, legal, political, socio-cultural and educational aspects and task environment that have a specific impact on business activities like customers, supplies of materials, labour, capital and work space, competitors for markets and resources and regulatory groups including governmental agencies trade unions and inter-firm associations. It has been observed that changes in the task environment affect only the entry of the innovative person into a particular field, but they do not help the making of the innovative person.

Entrepreneurship development (EDP) programmes acquire an importance as an effective human resource development tool. EDP is primarily meant for developing those first generation entrepreneurs who on their own cannot become successful entrepreneurs. It covers three major variables; location, target group and enterprise. Any of these can become the focus point for implementing an EDP. The remaining two will follow by making proper synthesis with the first. For example if the objective is to promote women entrepreneurs, suitable location and the proper entrepreneurial activities must match it. EDP in India has many objectives. An expert group constituted by NIESBUD accepted that it must be able to help selected entrepreneurs to develop and strengthen their entrepreneurial quality/motivation and to analyse environment related to small industry and small business. They must be able to select the product, formulate projects and understand the process and procedure of establishing small enterprises. They should also know the sources of help needed for launching the enterprise and acquire the basic management skills. Besides the above objectives of the programme there are other subsidiary objectives like enabling him to take strategic decisions and also enabling them to build an integrated team to fulfil the future demands. The future entrepreneurs should keep in mind the following aspects like technology and scope for modernisation, meeting quality requirements including ISO-9000, putting more emphasis on consumer satisfaction. He should also concentrate on energy conservation, environmental aspects, deduction in cost of production and must be prepared to face competition from both national and international angles. New opportunities are emerging in processing industries and in such areas like floriculture or software exports. The Government of India has also initiated policy measures for supporting first generation entrepreneurs through training and many state level and central level organisations are lending support to this programme. Even in the case of credit policies 40% of advances to SSI sector are reserved for tiny sector and village and cottage industries. An Entrepreneurship Development Institute had been set up for improving the entrepreneurial base for the north eastern region. Among other incentives 836 products are reserved for exclusive manufacture in the tiny sector and providing infrastructure support to entrepreneurial development institutes to augment their training capacities.

Among the various methods of entrepreneurship development in India five models have been experimented, SIET model was developed by SIET institute along with D.C. McClelland of Harvard University. This experiment is called as Kakinada experiment to verify the theory of achievement motivation in developing entrepreneurship. Six training experiments, each of two weeks duration were conducted during 1964-65 with 52 participants from Kakinada in Andhra

Pradesh, 26 participants from Vellore in Tamilnadu who had already set up SSI units. This experiment showed significant improvement in entrepreneurial performance of trainees. Later SIET also conducted training programme of 12 weeks duration in 1970. The follow up study in 1973 by SIET faculty had revealed that out of 155 potential entrepreneurs trained, around one half had either set up or in the process of setting up to their units. Further studies conducted by SIET disclosed the problems like procuring adequate raw material, delayed financial assistance and other problems faced by the trained entrepreneurs. Hence SIET had developed an integrated model of EDP in 1974. In this model the first stage stimulatory activities like education in business opportunities, identifying potential entrepreneurs, putting them in new product lines, making available to them techno-economic information and creating forums for entrepreneurs to discuss their problems will be under taken. The next stage is providing support activies that are intended to help entrepeneurs in setting up and commissioning the unit. In the third stage sustaining activities like continued association of all the supporting agencies to sustain and develop the enterprises will be initiated. Though the model encourages a sequencing of these activities, in practice all these can be initiated simultaneously.

Another model that has attracted attention is Gujarat model where it has incorporated in its EDP features like identifying potential entrepreneurs, assisting the training of entrepreneurs to prepare a viable project, developing entrepreneurial and managerial skills of training and providing them with financial and infrastructure facilities so that the new units are set up within the shortest possible time. This model has been initiated by Gujarat Industrial Corporation under its technician scheme which was later extended to non-technicians. In the case of the SIET model an important role is assigned to a local agency to initiate and support entrepreneurs besides the survey of the industrial prospects as an important input. But in the case of Gujarat model role of support institution is considered important.

Another model has been developed by entrepreneurship development of India which divides the general stages of EDP into three stages, namely pre-training, training and post - training. In the pre-training period selection of local trainer, creation of EDP awareness and identification of potential entrepreneurs as well as choosing training inputs will be the important aspect. In the second stage training will be given either as a six weeks full time programme or 12 week part time programme. Under this training programme behavioural inputs to develop personality traits will be provided in the first phase, technical inputs to provide guidance for project formulation will be given in the second phase and managerial inputs will be provided in the third phase. In the third stage of post-training, support involves follow up on loan application for finance, provision of infrastructure facilities and trouble shooting. Thus in this model the need for sustained follow up had been recognised due to the indecisiveness of some of the trainees to set up the new units.

Udai Pareek and Nandakarni presented in a role transformation models that would influence entrepreneurship. Their emphasis was on certain values and names which transform an individual into an entrepreneur. Other influences are the socio-culture traditions, sociopolitical economic policy and support systems. In the first phase the individual will be searching for a new identity and in a next phase an entrepreneurial alternative will be put into the mind of the individual. The identity formation requires the intervention by support organisation.

The Government Polytechnic, Ghaziabad, after analysing the existing design of the entrepreneurship development programmes had prepared a refined model for the unemployed technical persons. Apart from introducing the various aspects of entrepreneurship in the curriculum this model recomends a structured training through awareness camp by arranging a get together with established entrepreneurs. Further the follow up support from time to time should be extended by the training and placement cell. Besides these models there are forty agencies that are undertaking EDP work. Based on the Gujarat model the State Bank of India had conducted programmes for educated unemployed in industrially backward districts.

Studies had been undertaken on entrepreneurship and EDP highlighting the traits among entrepreneurs as well as a social pattern. For instance in one study one finding is that refugee entrepreneurs tend to be more innovative than local entrepreneurs. In another study economic factors are considered more important than there sociological factors. Another finding is that public enterprises have a low performance due to lack of entrepreneurial skills in the public sector. In studies conducted after 1980 the economic status of the father was found to be closely related to entrepreneurial success. In another study conducted in two coastal districts of Andhra Pradesh a majority of entrepreneurs were natives and belonged to upper class. Though they were having previous experience in the same field this level of education and the economic status were low. In a survey of 45 potential women entrepreneurs it was observed that women were attracted towards entrepreneurship due to getting more help and support. The need for achievement was moderate and the majority of them are from middle income groups.

The studies on EDPs showed that EDPs need fixing of priorities, follow up measures, spatial dispersal, training of trainees and a pattern for financing new ventures. A World Bank project on Gujarat innovation have showed that the programmes are effective and accelerating the development of small scale industries. Success in the ventures is the result of enterprise and competence rather than financial position of the entrepreneurs. In another study the adoption of extension approach by the support system had been advocated. The low success rate of entrepreneurship development programme has been attributed to the unsympathetic and often hostile response of the support system. In another study on programmes and progress made by SSI in ten Asian countries the concept of integrated entrepreneurship development had been suggested. In the next chapter the development of SSI sector in Andhra

Pradesh as well as studies on entrepreneurship in Andhra Pradesh had been examined. In the state of Andhra Pradesh the small scale industries contribute around 6% of gross state domestic product, and employ about 2.5 lakh people. The general policy towards the development of small scale sector is designed to develop entrepreneurship among women and disadvantaged groups. An examination of the trends in the development of industries in Andhra Pradesh will reveal the manner in which entrepreneurship had been fostered. The small scale industries, which have a pivotal role in generation of employment is mainly promoted by the District Industries Centre and at the state level the SSI board and development commission looks after the policy framework as well as the promotion and development of SSI. A comparison of the SSI units in 1973-74 and 1977-78 at the all India level reveals that a number of units had grown by about 7 times, while the value of their production had increased by about 6 times. Employment also registered a four fold increase while exports from this sector had increased by ten times.

In the state of Andhra Pradesh the number of units had increased by 3½ times while fixed investment had increased by 3½ times. Among the units set up in Andhra Pradesh, about half of the total units have been initiated in backward areas. The district development of industries, which also reflects entrepreneurial achievements in that district shows that in the case of medium and large scale industries Medak district occupies the first place followed by Ranga Reddy and Hyderabad. In the case of number of units set up in different districts as on 31-3-1996 in respect of total investments Visakhapatnam, comes first followed by Medak. In the case of employment Khammam stands first followed by Medak. Thus Medak, being very near to Hyderabad has generated entrepreneurial activities and in this sector 1433 units are operating with a total investment of Rs. 2519766.35 lakh and creating employment for 6.4 lakh. Among the various districts Hyderabad, Nalgonda are attracting more investments as there had been an increase in the number of units set up in these two districts in between 1995-1996.

Among the various lines of productive activity in the SSI sector, food processing has the highest share followed by mineral based industries and rubber, plastic and petroleum products. In the case of other lines of activity like chemical and allied industries, mineral based industries, basic metal industry, there is an improvement in their percentage shares out of the total units in 1999 over 1997. But in the case of employment there is an increase in the share in the case of textiles and rubber products.

In the case of the location of small scale units in different districts the highest percentage out of the total units of the state is to be found in Ranga Reddy followed by Hyderabad and Visakhapatnam as on 31-12-1999. Even in the case of relative shares of investment there is a big gap as slightly more than one fifth of the total investment is concentrated in Ranga Reddy while the investment in districts like Visakhapatnam, Krishna or Guntur is not even 1/15 of the total investment in the state.

One way to find the way in which entrepreneurship is being promoted in the districts is to assess the performance of DICs in reaching their targets. In between 1995-96 to 1999-2000 in districts like Anantapur, Cuddapah, Guntur, Karimnagar, Krishna, Kurnool, Mahaboobnagar, Medak, Nalgonda, Nizamabad, Prakasam, Srikakulam and Vizayanagaram, the achievements uniformly exceeded the targets in all the years. Among all the districts the performance of Guntur district is spectacular as it consistently over reached its target in the years 1997-98, 1998-99 and 1999-2000.

Entrepreneurship development is being fostered in the state of Andhra Pradesh by different institutions. A study had been conducted on emerging investors in East Godavari district by the Directorate of Industries of Andhra Pradesh in collaboration with ASCI Hyderabad . The study revealed some of the traits of entrepreneurs. A considerable number of entrepreneurs had some experience in the management of industries before they set up their own units and as such they were not new entrants to industry. A majority of them are middle aged and none of them had professional education.

Profit motive and the confidence that they can survive in the chosen line of production were the motivating factors and they are influenced in taking the decision for setting up of a unit by the advice given by their parents and family relations. A majority of the entrepreneurs had entered into the manufacturing sector due to the confidence that they have in their competence. The entrepreneurs were also influenced by their visits to other units and the minimum capital invested by them was Rs. 50,000 which had been their own money. The management of the unit was by the family members of the entrepreneurs with technical background in certain cases. A considerable number of them were planning to expand the operations and diversify into other products. About 25% of the units have reported the incidents of labour unrest in their units. As regards the financial assistance and other types of assistance the financial institutions are offering them different types of assistance.

Based on this survey they suggested certain recommendations like identification of profitable manufacturing lines by the department of industries and communicating the same to the entrepreneurs. New entrepreneurs should be given encouragement and there should be an extension in the range of services provided by the department Likewise confusion should be removed from the minds of the entrepreneurs on the sources of finance and other services and guided visits should be arranged for helping entrepreneurs. Another study conducted by SIET, Hyderabad also revealed similar findings. The respondents in this study were middle aged and a majority of them were Hindus and a relatively higher proportion among the entrepreneurs are degreeholders. The typical entrepreneurs either belonged to middle or low income group and a majority of them have urban orientation. The reasons for setting industrial units have been mentioned as economic gains, realising ambition, acquiring social prestige, and social responsibility. Those who have high adoption propensity realising the ambition was the most important reason for starting the industrial units. Risk taking ability did not influence the respondent for starting industrial units, while capital shortage and government red tapism were the most discouraging factors to start the industrial units. Among the respondents 80% visited office of the Directorate of Industries, 56% visited the Small Industries Service Institute, 20% visited the office of the DIC.

In Andhra Pradesh APIDC was set up not only to supplement financing function of APSFC but also to undertake promotional activities. It conducts industrial survey and obtains letters of intent and started manufacturing enterprises as its subsidiaries. It also became the agent of IDBI to channelise risk capital to the first generation entrepreneurs under the seed capital scheme besides undertaking the responsibility of distributing central and state subsidies. Another organisation that was set up was Andhra Pradesh Industrial Infrastructure Corporation to help the industrialists acquire well equipped sites for industrial establishments. The concept of joint sector had also been experimented where the APIDC executes projects with or without the private entrepreneurs. For instance until May 1987 the APIDC obtained 113 licences of which 62 were used and among these 62, twenty four were in joint sector. Though the Joint Sector enterprises were encouraged by the state, caste considerations and political affiliations have been the consideration for the identification of some of the private entrepreneurs that also partly led to the failure of some Joint sector enterprises. There were some notable successes also like Nagarjuna, Raasi and Standard Organics Limited. All these units have diversified into different lines of productive activity. In the new liberalisation scenario the A.P. government has introduced Andhra Pradesh Small Scale Industry (Development and Simplification of Procedures) Bill, 1998. This bill is meant for simplification of the procedures especially to help the entrepreneurs in the SSI sector. According to this bill, every entrepreneur who holds a provisional certificate in respect of small scale industrial unit may, within 6 months after the unit is commissioned can apply to the concerned industries development authority for the issue of a permanent certificate of Registration which can be issued without any delay. After the issue of the certificate each industrial unit shall be entitled to claim on a priority basis all the facilities and benefits that may from time to time be allowed to small scale or tiny industry. The financial assistance had also been liberalised and in view of the new lines of activity the strategy by APSFC will include identification of thrust areas such as electronics, computer software and hardware and also linear and non-linear computer animation, besides the traditional lines of productions.

According to the Vision 2020 the A.P. industrial sector is expected to grow at 11% a year and a total investment of roughly Rs. 11 lakh 65 thousand crores will be required three types of industries namely knowledge based, resource based and labour intensive industries include information technology, biotechnology and Pharmaceuticals; resource based industries include mining, construction and Agro-industries, while labour intensive industries include garments and leather products. These are defined as growth engines which are expected to contribute to the development small scale industries. The government is expected to foster entrepreneurship among women and disadvantaged groups. These groups will be given access to credit by the setting up of local area banks and exclusive banks for women. Further the entrepreneurs from disadvantaged groups will be offered fiscal concessions such as enhanced tax limits. APSFC has been financing special schemes like Mahila Udyama Nidhi, National Equity Fund, SEMFEX and women entrepreneur schemes. Besides APSFC, APIIC had also been expanding its activities to assist the entrepreneurs. It is now concentrating on industries specific parks like growth centres, export promotion industrial park and apparel export park. For instance, it is developing an industrial park at Parwada in Visakhapatnam by providing fiscal incentives. Likewise its latest venture in association with the central government is export promotion industrial park at Pashamylaram near Hyderabad. Another organisation that is striving to develop entrepreneurship is Andhra Pradesh Industrial and Technical Consultancy Organisation Limited (APITCO). Technical assistance is being offered by this organisation in such areas like computer software, tele-communications, cold storage, Bio-technology and even management of National and International seminars in Programmes like entrepreneurial development, management development and in other areas like energy audit programmes and conservation studies for industrial units. While it undertakes the training programmes in some of the above areas, it is also active in the promotion of appropriate and innovative rural technology. It had also been a catalyst in technology transfer in the area of edible oil refining, castor seed processing, and bulk drugs and chemicals. Thus a number of institutions are playing a significant role in fostering entrepreneurial development in the state of Andhra Pradesh. The socio-economic profile of the entrepreneurs chosen for a field study had been presented in the fourth chapter.

In order to understand the nature of entrepreneurship a questionnaire has been devised and administered to 150 small entrepreneurs operating industrial units in four districts of Telangana region in Andhra Pradesh, the four districts chosen for the study being Adilabad, Karimnagar, Khammam and Warangal. In the sample chosen for study there is a preponderance of entrepreneurs belonging to the age group of 26-45 years. Thus the middle aged have a greater representation in the sample. All the entrepreneurs are educated above SSC level and a majority of them are graduates. The caste-wise configuration shows that two thirds of the respondents, belong to other castes, while one fourth to the backward classes. The representation of scheduled castes is 6% and 2% represent scheduled tribes. Thus entrepreneurs from disadvantaged groups are also managing units in the study area. Among the respondents a very small percentage are from nuclear families, while a majority of the households have more than 8 dependents indicating that entrepreneurs have mostly originated from Joint families. As the parents' occupation has some relevance for entrepreneurship, an examination of family background shows that half of the respondents are drawn from business background, while one third belong to agricultural families. Entrepreneurship development programmes envisage the institutional support for the growth of entrepreneurs, but in the sample, institutions help to start a unit has been received by about one fifth of the respondents. In the case of the one third of the respondents the own initiative of the respondents has been the Prime movers for the setting up of the unit. Among others, for 14% the idea was given by the friends and in the case of 15% relatives and government agencies had a role. Thus in a majority of the cases either their own initiative or the help from friends made them to start a new venture. Among the respondents 72% received some training. As regards the line of production chosen by them food processing units has been chosen by a relatively higher number, while the next line of production is granite industries, of the total units 7% were started before 1980 but more than 70% were started after 1970. Thus a majority of the units are has a working life of 5 years.

A district-wise location of the sample units indicates that 50% are located in Khammam, 28.7% in Warangal, 13.3% in Karimnagar and 8% in Adilabad. Thus Adilabad has a relatively low percentage reflecting the backwardness of the district. The organisational setup of the units shows that 60% of the units are sole proprietorships, 36.7% are partnerships indicating that small units are organised in either of these forms. A majority of the units produce consumer goods while 25% of units produce intermediate goods. Thus a majority of the units are specialising in the production of consumer goods. The demand for the products produced by these units is reflected in the number of shifts operated by a unit and 50% of the units are operating two whifts and 32.7% are operating three shifts. Thus a majority of the units are utilising their plant and machinery in a more effective way. The installed capacity of the units is measured here in terms of their investment of the total units, 39.3% have installed capacity valued less than Rs. 25 lakh, 44.7% have installed capacity in the interval of Rs. 25-50 lakh; 33% are in the interval of Rs. 50-75 lakh, four units are investing more than Rs. 75 lakh. Thus a majority of the units have installed capacity valued less then Rs. 50 lakh. A chi-square test that the installed capacity among the units classified according to their capital structure is homogeneous had been rejected at 5 per cent level of significance. A majority of units that is 92% of the units employ more than ten workers per unit. The actual days functioned by the unit shows that many of the units functioning are for a longer period; especially 80% of the units are functioning for more than 50 days in a year. Investment in fixed capital by the sample units ranges from Rs. 5 lakh to more than Rs. 50 lakh, but a majority are investing more than. Rs. 50 lakh in fixed capital and the differences in the capital structure is significant and hence the chi-square test rejects the homogeneity hypothesis. The working capital requirements of the units show that there are certain units which have more working capital requirements than the fixed capital that they invested. A majority of the units have more than Rs. 5 lakh as their working capital requirement, and about 38% of the units are in need of more than Rs. 25 lakhs as their working capital. Thus the requirements of small scale units have also gone up due to the increased demand for their products in the market economy. As both fixed capital and working capital need the support from the institutional agencies, the respondents, were asked about the extent of help they were receiving from institutional agencies. Out of the total units 32% are not receiving any finance from the institutions, while 40% are receiving below 10% of their requirements and 15% are receiving in the interval of 10-15% while 7% of the units are receiving in the range of 15-20% and only 5% are receiving in the range of 20-25%. Thus institutional finance is not having a prominent role in their financial requirements. Among the units that received the institutional finance 50% received their financial assistance from SIDCO, while 20% received the assistance from APSFC.

The nature of financing shows that 38% received term loans; 20% received in the form of cash credit and demand loans were obtained by 8.7% of the units. Thus a significant proportion of the loans are in the form of term loans. Equity capital was raised only by 9% of the units while 17% depended on private finance. Among the various units 75% are approaching institutions for their working capital requirements. Here also the institutions are not completely providing the amount required by the units. Hence the gap between what they actually require and what is available to them indicates that about 60% of the units have less than Rs. 10 lakh as the gap. In the case of

14.7% of the units the gap is in the range of 25-50 lakh. Thus the socio-economic background shows that mostly middle aged, educated and having some business background have set up the the units and in a majority of the cases around 15 lakh had been invested in fixed capital and their representation is less in backward areas. Is some of the entrepreneurial aspects of the firms had been analysed in the fifth chapter.

Entrepreneurship has a major role in the efficient functioning of a firm and same of the aspects that contribute to the efficiency are modernisation of the firm, tapping the financial resources, sales growth, the markets in which the products are sold, utilising export promotion measures, and the profitability of the firm. Among the respondents 62% have said that they have replaced the machinery. As the capital structure of the firm has some association with the decision to replace the machinery and hence this response has been examined with respect to fixed capital as well as working capital. In the case of both fixed capital as well as working capital, the firms operating in the range 5-15 lakh a sizeable number could not replace their machinery. Another hypothesis is that educational attainment is positively convelated to the decision to replace the machinery. The data did not corroborate such a hypothesis as the proportion of those who replaced the machinery is much higher in the case of less educated entrepreneurs. Caste-wise differences show that in all castes those who had replaced the machinery were higher than those who did not and in the case of ST's all have replaced their machinery.

Among the various sources of finance it is usually presumed that internal surplus plays a prominent role in modernisation process. But in the case of this sample it is institutional finance that is playing an important role. Among the respondents 67.3% have expanded their capacity in the last five years and here also all the STs and two thirds of SCs have expanded their capacity; even among B.Cs it is 65% and it is 75% for O.C's. Thus among all caste groups a majority have expanded their capacity. When the expansion of capacity is correlated to the profit earning capacity of the respondents, units which are making profits in the higher range had generally gone for expansion of capacity in the last five years. A relatively higher proportion of the units are utilizing less than 10% of their internal surplus for expanding their capacity; on the other hand a considerable number can be found to depend for more than 10% of their requirements on institutional finance for expanding their capacity. But in the case of private finance about 1/3 of the total units are depending on private finance for 15% of their capital requirements.

When the entrepreneurs in the sample were asked whether they are planning either replacement or expansion of fixed capital in the next two years, 50.7% said that they don't have such plans, as the majority in the sample had already undertaken such an expansion. When this response was examined in association with the capital structure of the unit, those who have fixed capital in the ranges of Rs 25-50 lakh or above Rs. 50 lakhs have said yes in a considerable number. Thus as the investment of the units increases, the entreprenrus are willing to either replace the machinery or plan expansion of their units in the near future. Even in the case of firms having higher working capital requirements this finding was found to be valid. But one difference is that the units operating with working capital in the ranges of Rs. 5-15 lakh and Rs. 15-25 lakh have some constraints for expansion. Since profit earning capacity also influences a firm's capacity to expand, those earning profits in the range of Rs. 10-15 thousand, a higher percentage are willing to expand their firms. Thus very low profit earners and very high profit earners, in a relative sense are able to take the decision to expand their firms in the next two years.

The manner in which the different sources of finance will be utilised by the units for expansion in the next two years shows that a higher percentage of units would like to utilise a relatively higher proportion that is in the range of 10-25 from the institutional finance. Thus a considerable number would like to depend on institution finance. When caste-wise considerations are taken into account in the likely utilisation of finacnes from different sources, a very few that is two OC's and three B.C's, have said that they would depend on internal surplus for more than 25% of their financial requirements. In the case of institutional finance 15 O.C's one each from B.C's and SC's said that they would procure more than 25% of their requirements from institutional finance. In the case of private finance 48% of the respondents have said that they require it for less than 5%. In the case of adequacy of finances from financial institutions, more than two thirds of the respondents under each caste are satisfied with the provision of finances from institutions. Especially when they were asked to mention whether banks provided finance at the proper time, 66% have said that bank finance was given according to their requirements. But when a further probe was made whether there was any gap between their requirements and actual availability of finance, the gap between those who said yes and those who said no is more in the case of the above Rs. 50 lakh group of fixed capital investment. Again when they were asked whether they were receiving some help from the banks in the form of advice or in nursing their accounts such a help was rendered to those who are investing in fixed capital than to those who are having lower ranger of fixing capital. This signifies that the relatively weaker among the sample are not getting the required help from the institutions. A finding is that those who are having higher educational attainment could not get much help from the institutions. Higher educational attainment is naturally felt as an advantage to approach the bankers for assistance, but in the sample those who had a better educational attainment did not approach the bankers. Firms naturally accept deposits or loans from the public, but units utilising such sources are a few in the sample.

Entrepreneurship is naturally reflected in the ability of the entrepreneurs to improve the sales from year to year. A period of five years, that is 1993-1998, had been chosen to examine this phenomena. Firms had been improving their sales between one year and another year 38% were having their total sales value as less than Rs. 10 lakh in 1993. But this had become 0.7% in 1987-98. In the case of sales in the range of Rs. 10-20 lakh, there was an abrupt rise in the percentage of firms from 21.3 in 1996-97 to 32.7% in 1997-98. But in the next range of Rs. 20-30 lakh though there had been improvement in the percentage in the early years, it was only 2% rise in 1997-98 compared to 1996-97. Thus the firms having sales for less than Rs. 10 lakhs had declined and the overall improvement in the sales in different ranges of sales structure for a major number of firms is indicative of dynamic entrepreneurship.

Usually the firms sell their produce either on cash terms or on credit terms. Here 67.3% are selling on credit terms and the remaining on cash terms. In the case of credit the duration of the period for which credit will be allowed for below 30 days is found to be 41% of the firms; 4/5 ths of the respondents are charging wholesale price for their products. As regards the channels through which they sell their products about 1/4th sell directly to the consumers; about 1/3 rd market their products through retailers. Specialised wholesalers are utilised by 1/4 th of the firms for selling their products while the remaining are using distributors as their channel. While a majority of the units have their own sales organisations. The markets in which the entrepreneurs sell their product have been examined for the years 1995-96, 97, 1997-98, over the years the firms are selling a greater proportion of their output in the local markets. For instance in the case of the firms selling in the range of 50-75% the percentage of firms increased from 34 in 1995-96 to 45.3 in 1997-98. In 1997-98 there were two firms which were selling all their products in the local market only. A majority of the firms -97.3% were selling less than 25% of their total production within the state and this became 98% in 1997-98. Most of the firms were now concentrating on the national markets, as there had been improvement in the case of all the other firms in other higher ranges; there are five firms selling their total output within the country. A majority of the firms are exporting their products but they are exporting only less than 25% of their output. There is not much change in the number of firms that are exporting between 1995-96, and 1997-98. There are 20 firms engaged in export trade where the exports were more than 25% of their total output in 1996-97 as well as 1997-98.

Entrepreneurs were asked whether they were facing any competition from large scale units; the response was almost evenly divided. The reasons for such a competition were attributed to price differences by about 10% of the units, to quality differences by 17% but a relatively higher percentage, 36.7% attributed it to market practices. As regards export promotion schemes benefitting entrepreneurs only 1/4th of the respondents said that they were beneficial to them. Profit making capacity of the firm over the years 1995-96 to 1997-98 indicates that a majority of the firms could move from lower ranges to higher ranges. When a relationship with the capital structure is taken into account, the number is more in the lower ranges that is Rs. 5-15 lakh and Rs. 15-25 lakh for firms earning profits in the range of 5-10 thousand. But in 1997-98 the number of firms increased to 46. In 1997-98 we find the firms relative position changing for the firms earning profits in between Rs.10-15 thousand; thus in all the higher ranges of capital investment the number of firms declined, but the number increased in the next ranges of profits that is Rs. 15-20 thousand, Rs. 20-25 thousand and Rs. 25 thousand and above, for all categories of firms in fixed capital investment. In the case of working capital we find a different tendency except in the case of firms investing less than Rs. 5 lakh, in all other investment ranges the number had declined in 1997-98 compared to 1995-96 for firms earning profits in the range of Rs. 5-10 thousand. But in the case of Rs.15-20 thousand profit range, except for firms investing in the range of Rs. 15-25 lakh, the number increased in all other classes of working capital. Thus as the working capital is increasing the profits had also been increasing, the phenomenon being more prominent in the case of firms having working capital in the range of Rs. 5-15 lakh.

Profit earning may be also associated with the caste background. For instance in the case of OC's the number of those earning profits less than Rs. 5 thousand declined from 21 in 1995-96 to 3 in 1997-98, but at the same time the number increased from 27 to 37 in the next range of Rs. 5-10 thousand. Thus a considerable number from other castes could improve their profits even in other higher ranges of profits also. But in the case of BCs though there had been an increase in the number, it is not a substantial increase as only 4 could improve their position. In the case of B.C.s while none were there earning above Rs. 25,000 as profit in 1995-96, we find one firm in 1997-98 earning profits for more than Rs. 25,000. In the case S.C.'s though the number remained the same in Rs. 10-15 thousand profits range we find one firm earning profits in Rs. 15-20 thousand as well as Rs. 20000-25000 in 1997-98. In the case of ST's there is a change for one firm from Rs. 5-10 thousand range. There were two firms in 10-15 thousand range in 1996-97 as well as 1997-98. But one firm was earning about 25,000 in 1997-98 in a play all ST's could improve their position during the above period. When a comparison is made on the profit earning capacity of the entreprenrus based on their educational attainment, those who were educated upto S.S.C. could move from a lower range of profits to a higher range of profits. Likewise there was an improvement of the firms from middle categories to the last category, that is above Rs. 25,000. In the case of those who are educated upto 12th standard there is an improvement in reports learning between 1995-96 to 1997-98. In the case of graduates also we find an increase from 11 to 13 in Rs. 15-20 thousand and from 0 to 8 in Rs. 20-25 thousand. In the case of post graduates there had been a decline in the lower ranges of Rs. less than 5,000 and Rs. 10-15 thousand but an increase in all other ranges. This analysis shows that higher educational attainment need not be a decisive factor in earning profits. When a question had been asked whether they would like to continue in the same line of manufacture 68% have said yes indicating that they are a satisfied group.

In the next chapter the nexus between entrepreneurship and promotion of small scale industry had been done on the basis of the samples drawn from different districts. Among the various institutions that played an important role for setting up of the units, we find banks and DIC have a major role of the total units 1/3rd of the units received financial assistance from banks, but this type of assistance is having a higher percentage in Warangal. In the other districts DICs have a relatively lower percentage but a higher percentage is observed in Adilabad. As regards institutional assistance in the second phase almost 50% of the units received assistance from financial institutions. The next type of assistance is provision of electricity, among the four districts Khammam has better percentage than other districts. As regards the functions performed by the institutions, assistance for purchasing machinery had a relatively higher percentage in all districts except Warangal, while for fixed capital warangal had a higher percentage than other districts. When a question has been asked about the nature of institutions approach to small industry development it was considered as wholly helpful by a majority in Adilabad, while it was about 50% in the other three districts. It was mentioned payritally helpful by about 1/3rd of the units in Khammam, while occasionally helpful had a relatively higher percentage in Warangal.

When respondents were asked about their opinion regarding personnel engaged in training, 80% each in Khammam and Karimnagar replied in the affirmative. The percentage was slightly higher for Adilabad signifying the positive effect in a less developed district like Adilabad. When a further probe was made about the interagency cooperation among the institutions, the lowest percentage was noted in Adilabad indicating lack of inter-agency cooperation. As regards the sincerity of the institutions in promoting entrepreneurship a majority had a positive opinion. Likewise a majority were attracted to set up small units due to the encouragement given to them. To another question about the procedure for identifying potential entrepreneurs, 1/5th of the entrepreneurs in Karimnagar have attributed it to government policies, even for attributing it to training Karimnagar has a higher percentage than the other districts. In the case of cooperation of financial institutions the percentage is relatively high in all districts, while all the above reasons have been mentioned in a relatively higher percentage in Khammam and Adilabad. Thus financial institutions are able to the identify potential entrepreneur.

As regards the help and guidance provided to entrepreneur by institutions, more than 75% in each district said that they are helpful and even in the case of role played by the institutions in arranging electricity supply to the units, more than 70% in each district said it is helpful. In the case of assistance rendered by institutions regarding the marketing of the products a majority in each district, especially 90% in Khammam, expressed their opinion that they are receiving such assistance. For another question whether institutions are helping the units in the export of their products, a majority of the units said yes and here we can find 92% giving this response while it is 72% in Warangal. As regards the management consultancy services being provided to small entrepreneurs by the institutions, a majority have said that they are not being provided with such an assistance and this percentage is relatively higher in Warangal than in other districts, though in other districts also it is relatively high.

A number of institutions have been established to provide support to extension services to foster the entrepreneurship. When the respondents were asked about the nature of the services, a majority in each district have said that they were helpful. To a certain extent the DIC in each district is playing a prominent role in providing these extension services. As regards entrepreneurs experience with government officials a majority in each district considered them to be helpful. But in districts like Adilabad, Karimnagar, the response that they were not helpful is also relatively high when compared with other two districts. Thus in backward districts like Adilabad the officials should be more helpful for the growth of entrepreneurship. Likewise when asked about the role of agencies like IDA or other institutions fostering the growth of entrepreneurship, a majority of the entrepreneurs have said that their role was positive. When a question was asked about their survival in the highly competitive market economy under the present business environment, the opinion of the majority was that they can survive in their line of production at least up to 2010 while the other opinion was that they are able to utilise their capacity fully. Thus, the entrepreneurs are positive in their approach to the future.

Appendix - I

Facilities and Benefits Allowable to a Small Scale Industry

1) Any small scale industrial unit or any tiny industrial unit, in respect of which a permanent certificate of registration has been issued under this chapter, shall be entitled to claim on priority basis all the facilities and benefits, that may, from time to time, be allowed to small scale or tiny industry, such as. . .

   i) price preference in the matter of stores-purchases, by the Government departments or undertakings and quasi-government corporations;

   ii) Exemption from payment of ernest money deposit and production of the bank guarantees;

   iii) The lenient terms for furnishing collateral security for loans and other financial assistance towards working capital or otherwise, afforded by the banks included cooperative credit societies corporate financial agencies like Andhra Pradesh State Financial Corporation, Andhra Pradesh Small Scale Industries Development Corporation and development boards;

   iv) The rebates on interest on loans or financial assistance and the cash credit limits on loans to tiny industries and moratorium to be allowed initially for repayment of instalments for a short period of two or three years;

v) The concessional rates of premia for general insurance policies taken on plant and machinery, buildings and goods relating to small scale industrial units and for the life insurance policies taken by entrepreneurs and their employees;

2) Provided that the entrepreneurs belonging to the scheduled castes, scheduled tribes, backward classes and women shall be given first preference over others with regard to the matters specified above.

3) The Andhra Pradesh Small Scale Industries Development Authority may, from time to time, prepare, print and supply the entrepreneurs in the State a handbook, booklet, manual, brochure, severing or such other material for the information and use of the entrepreneurs, containing information as to...

(i) The latest orders, notifications, circulars or instructions of the State Government and the Central Government specifying the facilities and benefits allowed to the small scale industries;

(ii) The banks and other financial institutions which do not insist on collateral security in respect of loans sanctioned to the entrepreneurs and the interest, rebates and cash credits allowed to them;

(iii) The insurance companies dealing with claims of small scale industrial units affected by natural calamities which have fixed time limits for surveyor reports;

(iv) The income tax rebates or scales tax concessions allowed to tiny industries, and uptodate rates of taxes leviable on the small scale industries with special reference to the taxes levied in other States.

(v) The concessions in the levy of marketing cess, rural development cess, profession tax and the like in respect of small scale industries;

(vi) The refunds and exemptions and the removal of transport restrictions with regard to the products of small scale industries to be exported outside the State;

(vii) The reductions in tariffs on electric power supplied to small scale industries by the Andhra Pradesh State Electricity Board or other licensee, especially to tiny industries treating it as industrial consumption;

(viii) Tax exemptions or concessions allowed to entrepreneurs belonging to Scheduled Caste, Scheduled Tribe, Backward Class and Women and the small scale industrial units in the backward districts;

(ix) The supply of coal from Singareni Collieries and other raw-materials from main sources to the small scale industrial units;

(x) The marketing and supply of products of smallscale industries on rotation basis to the bulk consumers;

(xi) The training facilities available to the entrepreneurs;

(xii) The fixation of standards of quality of products of small scale industrial units and suggestion for improvement of such quality with particular reference to the testing, research and development facilities;

(xiii) The security measures to maintain law and order situation at or around the small scale industrial units at the time of any disturbance or anticipated disturbance;

(xiv) The criminal cases booked against the entrepreneurs withdrawn, in regard to offences and their disposal;

(xv) The advisory or coordinate committees constituted with representatives of small scale industries associations and workers unions for implementation of or change in, rules, circulars or other instructions;

(xvi) Any other matter pertaining to security of entrepreneurs, welfare of employees of small scale industrial units, development of small scale industries, rehabilitation or revival of sick small scale industrial units and technology and availability of products.

(b) The Authority may fix a nominal price, on the basis of no profit not loss, for any such hand-book, book, book-let, manual, brochure, souvenir or other material, saleable at the option of any entrepreneur other person.

Procedure Relating to Certificates of Registration for Existing Small Scale Industrial Units

1) Every entrepreneur who holds a valid provisional certificate of registration or a permanent certificate of registration in respect of his small scale industrial unit issued by or under the authority of the District Industries Centre prior to the date of commencement of this Act, shall, within thirty days from such date of commencement produce the provisional or permanent certificate of registration held by him before the District Small Industries Development Authority concerned for registration under the provisions of this Act.

2) Upon the production of the provisional or permanent certificate of registration under sub-section (1), the Authority shall, if satisfied that the said certificate is bonafide and in order and that the prescribed fees has been paid, register the said unit within thirty days from the date of such production of certificate and endorse on that certificate in the prescribed manner that it has been issued under the provisions of this Act.

3) All provisional or permanent certificates of registration issued to the entrepreneurs of small scale industrial units before the date of commencement of this Act and duly endorsed under this section shall be as valid and operative as if they have been issued under the provisions of this Act.

Simplified Procedure for Obtaining Approvals, Permissions, Licences etc., in respect of a Small Scale Industrial Unit

1) a) Every District Small Scale Industries Development Authority in relation to a small scale industrial unit registered under this Act be a single window agency for receiving, monitoring and overseeing the time bound disposal of all approvals, permissions, licences, consents and certificates or other sanctions required for the establishment, working and conducting of any such unit under the relevant law for the time being in force in the State.

b) It shall be the duty of every such Authority to obtain from the concerned officer and to furnish to the entrepreneur holding a provisional certificate of registration in respect of a small scale industrial unit any approval, permission, licence, consent, certificate or other sanction required under such relevant law, for the establishment, working and conduct of a small scale industrial unit in the district, within an aggregate period not exceeding four months from the date of receipt by the Authority of an application for the same.

c) The District Small Scale Industries Development Authority shall be under the superintendence and control of the Andhra Pradesh Small Scale Industries Development Authority, in exercising the powers, performing the function and discharging the duties conferred or imposed upon it under the provisions of this Act or the rules made thereunder.

2) Any entrepreneur holding a provisional certificate of registration in respect of a small scale industrial unit in a district shall make an application in the prescribed form and on payment of the fees prescribed under the relevant law or the rules made thereunder, to the concerned District Small Scale Industries Development Authority, in such manner and together with such documents as may be prescribed, for obtaining any approval, permission, licence, consent certificate or other sanction required under such relevant law for the establishment, working and conduct of a small scale industrial unit in the district.

3) As soon as may be after the receipt of the application under subsection(1), the Authority shall send the application to the concerned officer having jurisdiction over the area of operation of the small scale industrial unit, requiring him to examine the application and to advise the Authority whether, or not, to accord the necessary approval, permission, licence, consent, certificate or other sanction required under such relevant law and fixing a time limit of thirty days for sending his reply thereto.

4) Where the Authority receives the advice of the concerned officer for according the necessary

approval, permission, licence, consent, certificate or other sanction within the time limit fixed therefor, the Authority shall accord the same to the applicant under its authority; and thereupon such approval, permission, licence, consent, certificate or other sanction so accorded shall be deemed to have been accorded under such relevant law and shall be enforced accordingly.

5) Where the Authority is advised by the concerned officer to reject the application as being not bonafide or the particulars contained therein being not correct or complete or the fees prescribed for the application under the relevant law having not been paid, the Authority may after giving an opportunity to the applicant of making a representation against the rejection, or as the case may be, of correcting and completing the said particulars or complying with any other requirement, reject the application for reasons to be recorded in writing.

6) If, for any reason, the replay of the concerned officer is not received by the Authority within thirty days from the date of receipt of the application by the concerned officer or if no objections have been indicated by the concerned officer within the said period of thirty days, the Authority shall presume that the application is in order and accord the necessary approval, permission, licence, consent, certificate or other sanction to the applicant in respect of the small scale industrial unit and thereupon such approval, permission, licence, consent, certificate or other sanction shall be deemed to have been issued under the relevant law and shall be enforced accordingly.

7) Where an application is returned by the Authority to the entrepreneur for correction of certain defects or for completing certain particulars, the entrepreneur may resubmit the application after duly correcting

those defects and completing those particulars to the Authority within a period of thirty days from the date of return of the original application; and thereupon the provisions of this section shall apply to such resubmitted application as if it were a fresh application.

8) In this section-

a) The references to the term "approval, permission, licence, consent, certificate or other sanction required under the relevant law" shall, so far as may been be construed as references to the various approvals, permissions, licences, consents, certificates or other sanctions specified in column (2) of the Second Schedule;

b) The fees to be prescribed under sub-section(2) shall be in addition to the fees payable under any of the Acts specified in column (4) of the Second Schedule.

Amalgamation or Splitting up of Small Scale Industrial Units

1) Where an entrepreneur of a small scale industrial unit engaging in a particular activity intends to amalgamate his small scale industrial unit with any other small scale industrial unit of the same or similar activity, or where an entrepreneur of a small scale industrial unit of a particular activity intends to split it up into two or more small scale industrial units of the same or similar activity, thereby involving changes either in the organisational unit or units, as the case may be, the entrepreneur or entrepreneurs concerned shall intimate in writing of such intention to the District Small Scale Industries Development Authority concerned, in such manner, furnishing such particular and documents and on payment of such fees as may be prescribed.

2) Upon the receipt of intimation under sub-section(1), the District Small Scale Industries Development Authority concerned or where more than one such Authorities are concerned, each such Authority shall examine the intimation as to the genuineness of the intention of such intimation or the viability of the small scale industrial units after the intended amalgamation or as the case may be, of each of the units in the locality after the intended splitting up and if the Authority is satisfied that the intended amalgamation, or as the case may be, splitting up of the unit is bonafide and viable in the locality within the provisions of this Act, it shall, by an order, accord sanction to the entrepreneur or entrepreneurs for such amalgamation or splitting up, subject to such conditions as may be specified in the said order.

3) For the purpose of according sanction by the District Small Scale Industries Development Authority under this section, the Andhra Pradesh Small Scale Industries Development Authority shall formulate such norms as may be determined by it by regulations, having regard to the activity of the small scale industry, the locality in which the industrial activity of the amalgamated unit or split up units, is to be conducted and the financial and other aspects of the entrepreneurs concerned in relation to such unit or units.

4) All approvals, permissions, licences, consents, certificates or other sanctions subsisting and valid in respect of a small scale industrial unit or units, shall continue to be valid and in force in respect of the amalgamated unit, or as the case may be , split up units, until fresh approvals, permissions licences,, consents or certificates or other sanctions are accorded to the entrepreneur of the amalgamated unit or entrepreneurs of the split up units under the provisions of this Act:

Provided that any such continuance shall not extend beyond the period of validity specified therein.

Special Provisions in Respect of Certain Entrepreneurs

1) Where any person associated with a small scale industrial unit as a partner or otherwise, proposes with a view to set up a fresh small scale industrial unit on his own, while continuing or ceasing to be as such, he shall not be doniod registration of his small scale industrial unit, or any facilities or benefits including financial assistance available to an entrepreneur of any such unit, merely on the ground that the entrepreneur of the original unit is in arrears or that the original unit is not running on sound lines.

2) Where any person purchases a sick small scale industrial unit in an auction or otherwise with a view to revive the said sick unit on his own, such person, unless there is an agreement to the contrary, shall not be liable to pay any past liabilities attached to such sick unit such as, arrears of properly or land tax or electricity and water charges, but he shall be entitled to have all facilities for its revival and also to all the benefits available to an entrepreneur starting a fresh unit.

Explanation

The term "past liabilities" shall be construed as all the liabilities accused to the sick unit prior to the date of its purchase and taking possession by the purchaser.

Appendix - II

Andhra Pradesh State Financial Corporation is the prime term lending institution extending financial assistance to set up industrial ventures in tiny, small scale and medium scale sectors in Andhra Pradesh State. With the ongoing process of economic reform in India, there is good potential for setting up of new industrial ventures in Andhra Pradesh, more specifically in small scale sector. APSFC is preparing itself for taking right place in financing this sector.

Andhra Pradesh is a rich and prosperous agricultural state with abundant supply of raw materials and cereals. It is a leading producer of crops like tobacco, grounded, cotton, chillies, sugarane, jute, turmeric, etc. and large variety of fruits are produced in the sate. It is one of the major producers of milk in the country. Sericulture is another potential field. Due to the long coastline Andhra Pradesh is having pisciculture is being taken up in a great way. The state is very rich in coal deposits and second largest producer of barites in the world. Number of other minerals like, limestone, dolomite, iron are etc. are available in the state. It is rich in deposits of marble, granite and slate.

Thus, there is vast potential for development of industries based upon the natural resources available in the state.

Objectives of Policy for SSI Sector

The objectives of Corporation for development of SSI sector are as follows:

1. Accelerated industrial growth of the state in SSI Sector.
2. Increased employment generation.
3. Optimum utilisation of potential resources available in the state for industries development in SSI Sector.
4. Improve export potential.
5. Diagnose industrial sickness in small scale sector and assist the sick industries to recover from sickness.

Strategy for Development of Small Scale Sector

It is necessary to evolve a proper started to achieve the above objectives. The strategy proposed by the corporation is as follows:

1. To promote infrastructure for development of SSI sector.
2. To identify potential lines of activities and effect promotion of industries in these lines.
3. To create proper organisational arrangements.
4. To utilise funds available under various schemes like NEF, MUN, SC/ST component plan etc. for development of industries.
5. Simplification of procedures for quick sanction and timely assistance to entrepreneurs.
6. Conducting development companies and participating in entrepreneurs development programmes.

APSFC's Approach to Implement the Above Strategy is as Follows

1. To promote infrastructure for development of SSI Sector

The basic infrastructure facilities required for setting up

industries includes developed land, availability of power, labour, roads, water, raw materials and market. Presently APIIC is developing industrial estates in various growth centres. APSFC is intending to finance for entrepreneurs to develop private industrial estates where infrastructure facilities are made avail to set up various types of industries by the private entrepreneurs.

The Branch Manager/ Zonal Managers of the corporation are advised to identify the locations where there is scope for establishing private industrial estates.

APPFC is also advising entrepreneurs to utilise the infrastructures facilities already developed by APIIC and to set up industries in such estates.

2. *Identification of potential lines of activity and effective promotion of industries in these lines*

The corporation being aware of availability of abundant natural resources of the state, is in the process of indentifying the scope for various lines of activities to be established in different parts of the state be collecting the information available with the Government Organisations like, the commissioner of Industries, Department of Mines & Geology, Milk Commissioner, APLDDCF Ltd., Animal Husbandry, APEDC, Sericulture Department etc.

Based on the above information, the corporation intends to identify and encourage entrepreneurs for establishment of industries in small scale sector. Few of such lines includes poultry farming, floriculture, tissue culture, marine products, milk processing/pasturising/chilling units, slab polishing units, granite/marble cutting and polishing units both for indigenous and export markets, prawn feed mixing units, various agro/forest based industries/food industries, cold storage units, sericulture based industries, paper and paper products, lime and lime based industries, slag cement, products based on fly ash, clay and porcelain industries, pulverisation of minerals like quartz, feldspar, stonecrushing units, etc.

3. *To create proper organisational arrangements*

APSFC with a view to be closer to the needs of entrepreneurs and extend improved customers services, has decentralised its activities. It is now working on three tire system i.e. Branch set up, Zonal set up and Head Office. In this process, the Corporation has delegated sanction powers to all the Branch Managers to sanction loans upto Rs. 10,00 lakhs and all zonal managers to sanction loans upto Rs. 20.00 lakhs. All the disbursements, legal and recovery aspects are delegated to the Branch Managers to the maximum extent.

4. *Schemes for Weaker Sections*

Both Central and State Governments are giving emphasis for development of small scale sector by operating number of schemes. A few such schemes that can be quoted includes National Equity Fund (NEF) Scheme, Mahila Udyam Nidhi (MUN) Scheme, Scheme for Physically Handicapped, Scheme for SC/ ST entrepreneurs, Self Employment for ex-Servicemen (SEMFEX) Scheme, etc. In all these schemes, the promoters have to invest lesser margins compared to other general schemes. Under these schemes, entrepreneurs belonging to weaker sections of the society and who require upliftment are benefited or establishment of small scale units.

5. *Simplification of procedures for quick sanction and timely assistance to entrepreneurs*

APSFC by its decentralisation policy has streamlined the procedural aspects for sanctions and disbursement of loans for various entrepreneurs. It is endeavour of the Corporation that the service required to the entrepreneur be extended at the nearest point to him. The Organisation is tuned for good, effective and timely service to the deserved for establishment of their enterprises.

a) New schemes are evolved for improvement of the services to the industrialists. Under one such scheme, entrepreneurs are categorised as 'XO' category under, in which the industrial enterprises are at advanced stage of implementation and are sanctioned loans by giving special attention to such entrepreneurs and delay in processing or loan applications is reduced.

b) The Corporation has evolved another scheme by name "Good Entrepreneurs Scheme" under which the existing entrepreneurs who are prompt in repayment of earlier borrowing to the corporation are given special attention for expansion / diversification/ modernisation of their existing industrial activities and are also serviced quickly by extending interest concessions and relaxations in the promoters contribution. The Corporation is of the option that this scheme will be highly useful for industrial development and the quality of loan portfolio of the corporation is also improved.

c) By understanding the need for extending financial assistance for industrial units for captive power generation to overcome the operational problems involved due to the power cuts and power fluctuations, the corporation is considering loans for existing enterprises and such loans shall be precessed, sanctioned and disbursed at the corporation's branch officers. This facilitates industrialists to acquire DG sets and to overcome power problems by which the industrial units can be operated at their fullest capacity without interruptions.

d) The existing enterprises who are proposing to expand/ diversify their activity by purchases of machinery only are considered for financial assistance under Equipments Refinance Scheme.

e) For the benefit of small scale industries financed by the corporation has taken up new activities like Short Term Loans, Bill Discounting, etc. The Corporation is anticipating to introduce Hire Purchase and Equipment Leasing Activities also.

Thrust Areas

The strategy of the Corporation includes identification of thrust areas for promoting investment in small scale sector in the state. The following Thrush Areas have been identified after detailed analysis for scope for such unit in the state keeping in view, the availability of raw materials, market potential and other factors of production etc.

1. Agro based and food processing industries.
2. Pharmaceutical formulations.
3. Chemical and Chemical Based industries.
4. Electronics, computer software and hardware.
5. Mineral based industries.
6. Engineering Industry.
7. Plastics processing.
8. Linear and non-linear computer animation.

In order to encourage new investments in the above activities in small scale sectors, the corporation proposes for collection of information regarding potential for these industries.

Organisational Arrangements

The Corporation has clearly understood that the strategy for development of small scale sector can become a reality only proper organisational setup is evolved within the corporation. The corporation with its Head Office at Hyderabad is having 5 zonal offices located at Hyderabad, Warangal, Vijayawada, Tirupati and Visakhapatnam and 25 Branch Offices located at least one Branch Office in each district. The corporation is also having 2 field officers at Hindupur and Chittoor.

The Corporation is closely associated with the commissioner of industries and other industrial promotional organisations of the state Government for development of small scale sectors and duly coordinate themselves as a team.

Rehabilitation of Sick Industries

The Corporation is also giving its attention for rehabilitation of sick industrial units in small scale sector to avoid illness of the capital employed in these industries. The Corporation is having a separate department at Head Office for revival of sick small scale industries. The Corporation, after identifying the Cotentially viable sick industrial units and studying the reasons for their sickness, is trying to revive these units by extending concessions in the interest charged, rescheduling the term loan outstandings and funding the interest outstandings and also by sanctioning additional loans required for rehabilitation of these units.

The Corporation is keen in implementing the policy for development of small scale sector in the state. In this process, it is expecting cooperation from Government institutions, entrepreneurs and others. The development of small scale is reviewed periodically by the corporation and any hurdles in the process of development are being removed.

Appendix - III
Building Skills and Promoting Technological Development

To meet the growing need for skilled manpower in this section, the State will invest, as well as attract private investment, in vocational education and training by increasing the number of Industrial Training Institutes, polytechnics, engineering colleges, and other skill-building institutions.

The focus will be on ensuring that training in these institutions is oriented towards the needs of industry. This will be achieved in many ways. Advisory committees with representation from industry will be set up to advise on curricula, equipment on the job training, and campus recruitment. Practising entrepreneurs will be invited to teach or take some classes in training institutes. Finally, students will receive practical training in local industries.

The become globally competitive, the small-scale sector will have to invest in modernising and upgrading its technologies. This will be achieved through collaboration with research institutes; setting up a technology exchanged and setting up a technology development and modernisation fund.

- **Collaboration with research institutes**: Small Scale industries will interact closely with research institutes such as the Indian Institute of Chemical Technology, the Centre for Cellular and Molecular Biology, and the Institute of Tool Design, to upgrade their technology through the latest advances in knowledge in their segment. Since technology transfer to small units is currently restricted by the 24 per cent limit on equity participation by large units, the State will lobby the Government of India to increase this limit to limit to at least 49 per cent.

- **Technology exchange**: The Andhra Pradesh Technology Development Corporation will set up a technology exchange to provide information to small entrepreneurs about the latest technological developments worldwide, including the scope for technology transfer. The exchange will operate in close association with industry associations such as the Confederation of Indian Industry, consultants, and international organisations such as the World Assembly of Small and Medium Enterprises.
- **Technology development and modernisation fund**: The Small Industries Development Bank of India set up this fund in 1995. So far, small-scale industries in Andhra Pradesh have received Rs. 1.5 crore through this fund. Going forward, it will be given wide publicity to encourage more small-scale units to make use of this mechanism for securing funds.

PROVIDING INFRASTRUCTURE AND CREDIT

As in most other sectors, small-scale industry will need both basic and specialised infrastructure to achieve the growth envisaged. The initiatives to promote growth engines such as garments, knowledge-based services, and information technology will also benefit this sector. Thus, the theme parks, such as the Apparel Exports Park and Biotechnology Park (see Chapters 18 and 24) will provide infrastructure and infrastructure services to small - scale industries situteated in these parks, through their own or private investment. Providing captive mini-power plants, industrial water supply , roads, street - lighting, sanitation, etc., will be an integral part of this approach. Similarly , the provision of infrastructure, such as international airports, ports, warehouses, cold storage chains, cargo - handling facilities, and container services, will help to boost exports in the small-scale sector.

The Government will also encourage the setting up of private industrial estates to introduce competition in the provision of infrastructure services. Special facilities, such as clearances from the Pollution Control Board, Municipalities, the State Electricity Board, etc., will also be provided to these private estates.

A major impediment to the growth of small-scale industries is their lack of access to instillation credit. Faced with tighter capital adequacy norms and pressure to improve profitability, commercial banks are reluctant to lend to this sector and try to hedge their risk by insisting on collateral to fully cover loans. Furthermore, there are long delays in sanctioning loans.

The State Government will actively work with the Reserve Bank of India to ensure that small-scale units get adequate and timely credit. The Government will also ensure that the specific needs of this sector are met. This includes ensuring credit for the tiny and cottage industries sector and proving mechanisms for the meeting of dues to small-scale suppliers from defaulting large and medium units.

REFORMING POLICY AND SIMPLIFYING PROCEDURES

Policy restrictions and complex procedures greatly hinder the growth of the small-scale sector. Reforming policy and simplifying regulation are thus preconditions to boosting the growth of this sector.

Reforming Policy

The two major areas of reform would be fiscal concessions and labour law.

- **Fiscal concessions**: In 1996 liberal fiscal concessions were provided to all new industries, large, medium or small. As a result, older units are finding it hard to compete with newer ones and becoming sick. Moreover, these fiscal concessions are being misused in several ways. For instance, a unit coming to the end of a tax holiday period is declared sick and closed down. The same entrepreneur then registers a new unit merely to get the tax concession once again. Such fiscal incentives also lead to unhealthy competition between states, which offer all kinds of concessions, justifiable or not, to attract investment in their state.

The Government will revise its policy to remove these anomalies. In addition, to improve the competitiveness of the small-scale sector, it will seek a dialogue with other state governments, particularly those of the southern states, to rationalise fiscal incentives and curb unhealthy competition.

- **Labour Law**: The strength of small-scale units lies in their flexibility in production. The multiple labour laws, however , sometimes restrict this flexibility. These different laws need to be revised and combined into a single legislation. The State Government has already set up an Industrial Commission to study and recommend the consolidation of these laws and will pursue this issue with the Centre.

Simplifying Procedures

As for most industry in India, the setting up and operation of small-scale industries is severely hampered by the tangled web of procedures to be followed and clearances to be obtained. For small - scale industries, the most problematic procedures are the multiple registrations, certifications, and inspections required.

Some action has already been taken to address these issues. The Central Documentation and Clearance Centre (CDCC), set up in the Commissionerate of Industries, helps entrepreneurs obtain all the necessary clearances within a specific time and attaches an 'escort officer' to every project to follow up with Government departments. A voice - mail system has also been installed through which entrepreneurs can get information about the status of their applications. In addition, the Industrial Commission mentioned above will also work to simplify and consolidation procedures.

To rational the inspection process, the Government will allow accredited private agencies with a credible track record to undertake inspections and issue certificates.

Providing Assistance with Marketing

Small scale units also need assistance with marketing themselves and their product. The Government will provide this assistance indirectly by providing supporting infrastructure and opportunities for trade exchanges.

The Government will set up an International Trade Fair and large Convention Hall in Hyderabad. This centre will organise international exhibitions, fairs and conferences to help local industries market their products in international markets. The Government will also help small - scale units participate in foreign exhibitions and organise visits of oregin trade and industry delegations to Andhra Pradesh.

Furthermore, to encourage ancillarisation by large manufacturing units, the Government will organise vendor development programmes in major cities of the state.

Select Bibliography

Books

Abdul Hamid A.M., *Seminar on Small Scale Industries*, the Ernakulam District Small Industries Association, Cochin, April, 1970.

Anjaneya Swamy, G., *Agricultural Entrepreneurship in India*, Chugh Publications, Allahabad, 1989.

Akhouri Vinod and Gupta, M.M.P., *Sustaining Entrepreneurship*, (Seminar Proceedings). NIESBUD, 1990.

Ashok Kumar, S., *Entrepreneurship in Small Industry*, Discovery Publishing House, 1990.

Awasthi, Dinesh N. and Jose Sebastian, *Evaluation of Entrepreneurship Development Programme*, Sage Publications, New Delhi, 1996.

Assistance. A. I. D., *Small Scale Industries in India*, The National Small Industries Corporation Ltd. (A Govt. of India Undertaking, New Delhi), 1966.

Akram, S., *Development of Small Scale Industries in Bihar*, Capital Publishing House, Delhi, 1984.

Basu, S. K., *Place and Problems of Small Industries*, Mukherjee & Co. Private Ltd. Calcutta, 1957.

Balakrishnan, G., *Financing of Small Scale Industries in India (1950-52)*, Gokhale Institute of Politics & Economics, Pune.

Bedapati Mohanty, *Economics of Small Scale Industries*, Ashish Publishing House, New Delhi, 1986.

Berna, J.J., *Industrial Entrepreneurship in Madras State*, Asia Publishing House, Bombay, 1960.

Bose, A.N., *Calcutta and Rural Bengal: Small Sector Symbiosis*, Minerva Associates (Publications) Pvt. Ltd., 1978.

Chebbi, V.K., *Capital Requirements of Small Industry*, Small Industry Extension Training, Hyderabad, 1974.

Chee Peng Lim., *The Role of Small Industry in the Malaysian Economy*, Faculty of Economics and Admis. University of Malaya, 1975.

Chee Reng Lim, M.C. Purthucheary & Donald Lee, *A Study of Small Entrepreneurs and Entrepreneurial Development Programmes in Malaysia* (An Adipa Research Project) Faculty of Economics and Administration, University of Malaya, Kuala Lumpur, 1978.

Clifford, M. Baumback, *Baumback's Guide to Entrepreneurship*, Prentice Hall Inc., 1981.

Development Commissioner, Small Scale Industries, *Entrepreneurship Development Programme*, New Delhi. Govt. of India Press, 1977.

David Silver, A., *Entrepreneurial Megabucks*, John Wiley & Sons, New York, 1985.

Desai, Arvind N., *Environment and Entrepreneur*, Ashish Publishing House, New Delhi, 1989.

Drucker Peter, F., *Innovation Entrepreneurship: Practice and Principles*, Pan Books, London, 1986.

D.D. Mali, A.R. Baruah & NISIET Guwahati, *Emerging Entrepreneurship in North East India* (Third Select cases), Govt. of India, North Eastern Council Secretariat, Shillong, 1992.

Entrepreneurship Development Institute of India, Ahmedabad,

Developing New Entrepreneurs, Sahity Mudranalaya, Ahmedabad, 1987.

EDII, *A Handbook of New Entrepreneurs*, Entrepreneurship Development Institute of India, Ahmedabad, 1986.

Elizabeth Hennessy, *The Entrepreneurs*, S Cope Books, 1980.

Eugene Stalley and Richard Morse, *Modern Small Industries for Developing Countries*, McGraw Hill Book Co., New York, 1965.

Gautam Vinayshil, *Technical Entrepreneurship. Issues of Research and Application*, Global Business Press, New Delhi, 1992.

Gorden B. Baty, *Entrepreneurship Playing to Win*, Prentice Hall, Inc., 1979.

Government of Andhra Pradesh: *Vision-2020*.

Government of India, *Report of the International Perspective Planning Team*, Development of Small Scale Industries in India, 1973.

Government of India, *Development of Small Scale Industries in India Prospect, Problems and Policies*, Report of International prospective planning team on Small Industries, Ministry of Commerce & Industry, Govt. of India, 22nd July, 1963.

Government of India, *Report of the Committee on Development of Small and Medium Entrepreneurs*, India Investment Centre, New Delhi, 1986.

Gordon. B. Baty, *Entrepreneurship for the Eighties*, Reston Publishing Co., 1981.

Government of India, *Development of Small and Medium Entrepreneurs*, Ministry of Industrial Development, New Delhi, 1973.

Government of India, Economic Survey, 1995-96.

Hadimani, R.N., *Dynamics of Industrial Entrepreneurship*, Ashish Publishing House, New Delhi, 1985.

Holt, David H., *Entrepreneurship*, Prentice Hall of India, New Delhi, 1998.

Habidur Rahman, A.H.M., *Entrepreneurship and Small Enterprise Development in Bangladesh*, Bureau of Business Research, University of Dacca, 1979.

Honstadt, *Entrepreneurship*, Lord Publishing, New Delhi, 1985.

Ichiro Oshikawa & Kenzo Ototake, *Outline of Policy for Smaller Enterprises, Japanese Experience*, Asian Productivity Organisation, August 1969.

John, A. Horhaday, Jeffry A. Timmons & Karl, H. Vesper, Frontiers of Entrepreneurship Research, Sponsored by Babson College Centre for Entrepreneurial Studies, Wellesly, Massachusetts 1981, 82, 83, 84, 85.

James, J. & Berna, S.J., *Industrial Entrepreneurship in Madras State*, Asia Publishing House, Madras, 1960.

Kathayini, J., *A Study on Entrepreneurial Attitudes of Students*, Unpublished Thesis, S.V. University, Tirupati, 1999.

Kent, Calvin A, Doneld L. Sexton and Kerl H. Vesper (ed. s): *Encyclopedia of Entrepreneurship*, Prentice Hall, New Jersey, 1983 .

Kilby, Peter, *Entrepreneurship and Economic Development*, Free Press, New York, 1971.

Krishna Swamy, K.S., *Seminar on Financing of Small Scale Industries in India*, Reserve Bank of India, 1965.

Krishnalal Sharma, *Entrepreneurial Performance in Role Perspective*, Abhinav Publications, New Delhi, 1975.

Laxmana Rao, V., *Industrial Entrepreneurship in India*, Chugh Publication, Allahabad, 1991.

Leon v Chico, *Small Enterprise and Entrepreneurship Development in Eleven Asian Pacific Countries*, Technonet Asia and Singapore, 1983.

Manimala, Mathew J., *OBS for Social Transformation*, Sage Publications, New Delhi, 1999

Manimala, Mathew J., *Entrepreneurship Theory at the Cross Roads*, Wheeler Company Ltd. 1999.

Mark Blaug, *Economic Theory in Retrospect*, Cambridge University Press, 1997.

Madhu Murthy, K., "Some Aspects of Entrepreneurship Development in Developing Economies with Specific Reference to India", unpublished Ph.D. Thesis, Kakatiya University, Warangal, 1997.

McCelland, D.C., *The Achieving Society*, D. Van Nostrand, Princeton, New Jersey, 1961.

McCelland, D.C. and David G. Winter, *Motivating Economic Achievement*, Free Press, New York, 1971.

Michael, J.C. Martin, *Managing Technological Innovation and Entrepreneurship*, Reston Publishing Company Inc. Reston, Virginia, 1984.

Ministry of Industry & Company Affairs, New Delhi, *District Industries Centres Programme Physical Achievements*, Small Scale Industries of the Development Commissioner, 1983 - 84.

Ministry of Industry & Civil Supplies, *All India Report on Census of Small Scale Industries*, Development Commissioner Small Scale Industries, June 1976.

Malcolm Harper and Tan Thasam Scan, *Small Enterprises in Developing Countries, Case Studies and Conclusions*, Intermediate Technology Publications Ltd., London, 1979.

Mark Casson, *The Entrepreneur: An Economic Theory*, Martin Robertson, 1982.

Nanjundan, S., Robinson, H. E. & Eugene Stanley, *Economic Research for Small Industry Development*, Asia Publishing House, Madras, 1962.

Nagendra P. Singh, *Entrepreneurship Development: Theories & Practice*, Inter Cultural Foundation for Development Management, Govt. of India Press, Delhi, 1985.

Nafees Baig & Mohd. Asif Ali Khan, *Entrepreneurship and Business Environment*, Ashish Publishing House, New Delhi, 1990.

Narendra, S.S. Risht & Pamila, K. Sharma, *Entrepreneurship Expectations and Experience*, Himalaya Publications House, New Delhi, 1991.

Owens, Raymond Lee, *The New Vaisyas*, Allied Published Pvt. Ltd, Ashish Nandy Bombay, 1977

Organisation for Economic Cooperation and Development: *Promotion of Small and Medium sized firms in developing countries through collective action*, Organisation for Economic Cooperation and Development, Paris.

Pakki Reddy, *Industrial Promotion through Joint Sector: A Study in Andhra Pradesh*, a Ph.D. thesis, Osmania University, 1990.

Pathak, H.H., *Problems of Small Scale Entrepreneurs*, Industrial Development Bank of India, 1975.

Patel, V.G., *Entrepreneurial and Economic Profile of a Small Scale Unit*, Gujarat Industries Corporation, Ahmedabad, 1975.

Patel, V. G., *Innovation in Banking: The Gujarat Experiments*, IDBI, Bombay, 1981.

Patel, V. G., *Entrepreneurship Development Programme in India and its Relevants to Developing Countries*, EDII, Ahmedabad, 1987.

Philip, A. Neck and Robert E. Nelson, *Small Enterprise Development: Policies and Programmes*, ILO, Geneva, 1987.

Rathore, B.S., Dhameja, S. K., *Entrepreneurship in the Twenty First Century*, Rawat Publication, Jaipur, 1999.

Ramakrishna, P., *New Entrepreneurship in Small Scale Industry in Delhi*, Economic and Scientific Research Foundation, New Delhi, 1975.

Rano, T.V. & Manlik, T. K., *Identification and Selection of Small Scale Entrepreneurs*, IIM, Ahmedabad, 1979.

Ravi Chandra, *Entrepreneurial Success: A Psychological Study*, Sterling Publication Pvt. Ltd., New Delhi, 1991.

Richard Scarze & Robert Goffee, *The Entrepreneurship Middle Class*, Croom Helm, London, Canberra, 1982.

Richard Mansfield et al., *The Identification and Assessment of Competencies and Other Personal Characteristics of Entrepreneurs in Developing Countries*, McBer & Co, Baston, 1987.

Robert & C. Ronstadt, *Entrepreneurship*, Lord Publishing, Madras, 1984.

Radha Krishnan, R., *An Evaluation of Entrepreneurship Development Programme in Tamil Nadu*, Ph.D. thesis, Kakatiya University, 1994.

Ram Sagar Singh, *Rural Elite Entrepreneurship and Social Change*, Rawat Publication, 1985.

Ram, K. Vepa, *Small Industry Development Programme*, Indian Institute of Public Administration, New Delhi, 1983.

Saini, J.S. & S.K. Dhameja (ed.), *Entrepreneurship and Small Business*, Rawat Publications, Jaipur, 1998.

Schumpter, Joseph A., *Capitalism, Socialism and Democracy*, S. Chand & Co, New Delhi, 1980.

Subarna, M.C., *Entrepreneurial Development Programme for Bihar*, Bholanath Industries, Patna, 1974.

Sharma, *Entrepreneurial Performance in Role Perspective*, Abinav Publications, New Delhi, 1975.

Sharma, D.D., Dhameja, S.K. & Gunjan, B.R. (ed.), *Entrepreneurship Management and Globalisation*, Rawat Publications, Jaipur, 1999.

Singh, P.N., *Development Entrepreneurship for Economic Growth*, Vikas Publishing, 1986.

Sharma, R.A., *Entrepreneurial Change in Indian Industry*, Sterling Publishers Pvt. Ltd., 1980.

Sharma, R.A., *Entrepreneurial Performance in Indian Industry*, Inter-India Publication, New Delhi, 1985.

Sharma, S.V.S., *Small Entrepreneurship and Enterprise Growth*, Seema Publications, 1985.

Sharma, S.V.S., *Small Entrepreneurial Development in Some Asian Countries: A Comparative Study*, Light & Life Publishers, 1979.

Sharma, S.V.S and Akhourim, M.P., *Small Entrepreneurial Development—Indian Experience in North Eastern Region*, SIET, Hyderabad.

Sharma, S.V.S. et al. (ed), *Development to Entrepreneurship, Issues and Problems*, SIET, Hyderabad, 1980.

SIDBI, *Report of on SSI Sector*, 1997-98.

Shiva Ramu, S., *Entrepreneurship and Enterprise Growth*, Seema Publications, 1985.

Small Industry Extension Training Institute, Hyderabad, *Small Entrepreneurial Development in North Eastern India*, Government of India, Hyderabad, 1978.

Small Industries Extension Training Institute, *Socio-psychological Factors Influencing the Adoption or Starting of a Small Industry Unit: A Research Study*, Small Industry Extension Training Institute, Hyderabad.

Thanulingam Nadar, N., *Small Scale Industry Inter-relationship with Large Scale Industry*, Rainbow Publication, Coimbatore, 1985.

Vasant Desai, *Entrepreneurial Development*, Volume 1, 2 and 3, Himalaya P ıblishing House, New Delhi, 1996.

William Copulsky & Herbert. W. McNutty, *Entrepreneurship and the Corporation*, A Division of American Management Association, 1974.

William Naumes, *The Entrepreneurial Manager in the Small Business*, Addison Wesley Publishing Company, London, 1978.

Zafar Ataf, *Pakistani Entrepreneurship*, IBD Publishing and Distribution, 1984.

Articles

Ponnalal, "States of small scale enterprises in Industrial estate in Andhra Pradesh, A study" *SEDME*, vol. 21, No. 4, Dec. 1994.

Rao, N.K.A., *Entrepreneurship Development - 2001*, National Social Science Documentation Centre, (ICSSR), New Delhi.

Siddharth Das, "Entrepreneurship in the 21st century", *Indian Management*, June, 1999.

Venkatapathy, R., "Cognitive self among First generation entrepreneurs and second generation Entrepreneurs," *EDME*, vol. xvii, Dec. 1991.

Reports and Brochures

Small Scale Industries in India, 1999.

APSFC Scheme for financial assistance 1999.

APSFC Lending Policy 2000 - 2001.

Andhra Pradesh Industrial and Technical Consultancy Organisation Ltd., Brochure on one with entrepreneur.

APIIC & A.P. Industries Infrastructure Corporation, Brochure on Industrial Park, Parwada.

Index

❏❏❏